Walkers', Cyclists' and Horse Riders'

LightFoot Guide to the Via Francigena

Edit

Bes

V

453

ISBN: 978-2-917183-07-6

Riding the Milky Way - Long Riders' Press 2006
Riding the Roman Way - Pilgrimage Publications 2007
Reflections - A Pictorial Journey Along the Via Francigena 2008
LightFoot Guide to the Three Saints Way - Winchester to Mont St Michel 2008
LightFoot Guide to the Three Saints Way - Mont St Michel to St Jean d'Angely 2008

The authors have done their best to ensure the accuracy and currency of the information in this LightFoot Guide to the Via Francigena, however they can accept no responsibility for any loss, injury or inconvenience sustained by any traveller as a result of information contained in the guide. Changes will inevitably occur within the lifespan of this edition and the authors welcome notification of such changes and any other feedback that will enable them to enhance the quality of the guide.

Porte Noir, Besançon

Jannina Veit Teuten, born in London in 1939, gained the National Diploma in Design at Twickenham Art College (1960). She then moved to Florence, Italy (1970), and studied painting and sculpture at the Accademia delle Belle Arte in Florence (1971 to 1980). She is primarily a painter of portraits in oils, but her first water colour exhibition, on request, was of Settignano (1980). Many more followed in England, France and Italy. One, of major importance was to commemorate the 80th Anniversary of the battle of the Somme in Picardy and 30 views of recent urban restoration in Amiens. Work for the Via Francigena project began in 1993 - 23 exhibitions of paintings staged from Canterbury to Rome. From 2002, Jannina has exhibited paintings of interiors and portraits, in oils, in Tuscany, and has had repeat showings of the Via Francigena Project in Italy. In 2006, she was Commended and ministerial level for her work to promote the project. Work in progress: water colours and drawings of the Via Francigena south of Rome for a permanent exhibition due to be launched in 2010.

Tel: 0039 349 17 06 874 veitteuten@hotmail.it

Pilgrimage Publications is a not-for-profit organisation dedicated to the identification and mapping of pilgrim routes all over the world, regardless of religion or belief. Any revenue derived from the sale of guides or related activities is used further to enhance the service and support provided to pilgrims.

Pilgrimage Publications has been created by Paul Chinn and Babette Gallard, two people who have covered many hundreds of pilgrim kilometres. The ethos of their operation is based on 4 key aims:

1. *To enable walkers, cyclists and riders to follow pilgrim routes all over the world.*
2. *To ensure Pilgrimage Publications guides are as current as possible, using pilgrim feedback as a major source of information.*
3. *To produce LightFoot Guides or any other materials using only the most environmentally friendly option currently available.*
4. *To promote eco-friendly travel.*

Tracing Yesterday Using Today's Technology

LightFoot Guides are designed to enable everyone to meet their personal goals and enjoy the best, whilst avoiding the worst, of following ancient pilgrimage routes. Written for Walkers, Cyclists and Horse Riders, every section of this LightFoot guide provides specific information for each group.

LightFoot Guides provide metre-by-metre instructions based on GPS co-ordinates, supported by Online Updates and produced by using the Print On Demand method - the most environmentally friendly option currently available.

The authors would like to emphasise that they have made great efforts to use only public footpaths and to respect private property. Historically, pilgrims may not have been so severely restricted by ownership rights and the pressures of expanding populations, but unfortunately this is no longer the case. Today, even the most free-spirited traveller must adhere to commonly accepted routes. Failure to do so will only antagonise local residents, encourage the closure of routes and inhibit pilgrims following on behind.

Revised editions of this guide will be published each year, but everyone is advised to refer to the relevant update page on the Pilgrimage Publications website - changes will be listed as soon as they are received.

Please let us know about any changes to the route or inaccuracies within this guide book - mail@pilgrimagepublications.com

Our special thanks go to:
Barbara Edgar, for her tireless and ever vigilant proof-reading
William Marques, Confraternity of Pilgrims to Rome, for his help and support
François Louviot, President Association Via Francigena Français, for his support and offer of accommodation information
Giovanni Caselli, for his thoughtful foreward to our guide
Jannina Veit Teuten, for the use of her evocative and beautiful watercolours

CONTENTS **Page**

FOREWORD - Giovanni Caselli has been a Fellow of the Royal Anthropological Institute of Great Britain (1972), and a Member of the Institute of Archaeology of Great Britain (1985). He is the author and illustrator of many history books for young adults and as an expert in the history of land communications and settlement has lectured on the subject at the Institute of Archaeology of London, at the University of Malta and in Italy.

Via Francigena - RIVER OF HISTORY

"Roads are the rivers of history", I remember reading this in a book when I was very young and beginning to become interested in history. Equally one may say that roads are the bloodstream of nations. People, goods and most of all ideas, have travelled along roads and all these have left their mark.

"All roads lead to Rome", is an old saying, but not only in the Italian tradition. Even nations which were never part of the Roman Empire have it. After St. Augustine of Canterbury converted the Saxons, several of their kings made the journey to Rome. Some of them died there, and a special section of the Vatican became a Saxon enclave for visitors from Britain. From then on and until the Reformation, the Pope's guards were all Saxons. Saxon Archbishops had to go to Rome for their official investiture when they received the "pallium", an ecclesiastical vestment, from the Pope himself.

There are many early medieval records of kings (among them King Alfred and King Cnut), abbots (like Ceolfrid of Wearmouth and Jarrow), Irish saints (like Saint Columbanus of Bobbio), and Canterbury archbishops going on a journey to Rome, but only one such record enables us to reconstruct the route and, of course, put it on today's map and travel it. Archbishop Sigeric of Canterbury, an otherwise obscure figure, barely making a minor appearance in British history, recorded his return journey from Rome, and this document, dating to the 10th Century, still survives. William Stubbs, a 19th century English historian, discovered Sigeric's account of his journey from Rome which took place in 990-992, and transcribed it, interpreting the 80 place-names, or submansiones of the route, where the prelate and his entourage spent their nights,

In 1985, as the millennium anniversary of this journey approached, I thought of trying Sigeric's route to see what the expert eye could detect on the banks of that "river of history". And, as always happens, the experience on the ground was full of unexpected surprises. I will never forget the excitement of this true journey through space and time, from Canterbury to Rome. It was not so much the great cities, like Laon or Rheims, but the smallest villages or farms, which reserved the greatest surprises for the time traveller. In France I discovered barns that had been Templar's chapels and old houses called "hospital" (meaning hostel). The road through the Marne, between Rheims and Chalons-en-Champagne, known as the Voie Romaine, looked as if the Romans had just left it and then, as if that were not exciting enough, I discovered the Chausseé Brunehaut - a term which in Northern France identifies a Roman Road, and in popular tradition also signifies that it is a road built by "Queen Bruhehilde, wife of Julius Caesar"!

In Switzerland, I came across ruins of Roman villas with splendid mosaics, while the Saint Bernard Pass itself is practically a museum. The original Roman road, cut deep in the rock and bearing deep ruts, can be walked for some hundreds of yards. During the Dark Ages English pilgrims were attacked by the Saracens who, for a time, controlled the pass. From there and across the Italian border, Roman bridges and Roman milestones can be seen in every village all the way down to Aosta - a splendid little town with massive ruins towering above the modern buildings and ancient monasteries of Sigeric's time, founded by Irish saints. Vercelli and Santhià, are Roman and medieval treasure troves. The "Vercelli Book" in the Cathedral Library -one of the oldest of the four Old English Poetic Codices - is an anthology of Old English Prose and verse dating back to the late 10th century.

From here the River Po was crossed at a place where a ferry has now been put back into service for the benefit of modern pilgrims, thanks to the advice I gave to the local people. In Fidenza, the great Romanesque and Gothic cathedral of the small town depicts friezes with rows of Via Francigena pilgrims that give us a very good idea of what the travellers of the 12th-13th century looked like on the road. Over the Apennines I also found fantastic Romanesque artworks and roads frequently called Via Romea – the medieval name of any road leading to Rome.

The Via Francigena in Tuscany is, in my view, the most evocative. Lucca was rebuilt by an Irish saint, St. Finnian, in the 7th century on the ruins of the Roman city and the town was subsequently administered by an Irish nun for a good part of the 8th century. After Lucca, having crossed the Arno, the road takes travellers to the excavations of San Genesio, just below San Miniato, a lost city whose cathedral is now only a trace in a sunflower field.

Then onto San Gimignano and Siena, two locations that do not require any further description from me, except perhaps to add that they both owe their existence to medieval traffic along the Francigena, where it was crossed by the droves of shepherds going to the coast from the Apennines. Siena grew rich by renting the grassland of the Maremma in Winter. The oldest bank in Italy, Siena's bank, Monte dei Paschi di Siena, literally means "Savings from the renting of pastures". The greatest painter of Siena, Simone Martini was a Frenchman from Tours.

After Siena the road winds among the rolling hills of Val d'Orcia, and you feel as if you are walking in a dream or a timeless world painted by a surrealist artist. Then come the ragged vast landscapes between Monte Amiata and Radicofani, where in Sigeric's times there was just one inn called "Mala Mulier" (Dishonest wife). Here, in about 715, two monks from Wearmouth and Jarrow vanished. They were carrying the largest illustrated book ever produced as a gift for the Pope - a Bible made of the skins of 1500 calves, and needing a pack mule to carry it. In the 16th century, a large book was bought by the Medici library from the monks of San Salvatore of Mount Amiata for their library in Florence and in the 19th century, scholars discovered that that book was the English book described by the Venerable Bede. Further south, the Via Francigena enters the flat tuff plateau of Lazio and retraces the Roman Via Cassia. After walking through the town and on the rim of Lake Bolsena, the traveller will taste the fine wine of Montefiascone , which induced even a pope to say "it is, it is, it is of the best".

After all of this, the modern pilgrim will finally tread shiny Roman paving stones, skirting vast Roman ruins and, after visiting but then leaving aside the town of Viterbo, he will cross streams on Roman bridges, feel the proximity of Rome and ultimately reach Mons Gaudii" (a vantage point thus named by pilgrims from before Sigeric's times) from which he will see the Holy Dome of St. Peter's and the Vatican .

At the journey's end the traveller will be a richer person, elevated by the experience and the acquisition of knowledge obtainable only by sailing along this "river of history" .

For more information about Giovanni Caselli go to:

http://www.giovannicaselli.com
http://www.giovannicaselli.it
http://www.giovannicaselli.it/LA%20VIA%20ROMEA%20PAGE%201.htm
http://www.donsmaps.com/caselli.html

The idea of sacred motion or travel runs deep in human religion, dating back to when early humans would climb hilltops to be closer to God or go to a specific spot to dance around in circles. Spiritual talk is full of the language of travel : walking the walk, leaving behind, stepping forward and following God's paths on our spiritual journey of life. Christian pilgrims have travelled across Europe since medieval times and for a variety of reasons. The majority would have been heading for three main sites of devotion, mostly on foot, covering anything up to 20 or 30 kilometres a day and usually carrying one of the three pilgrimage emblems: a scallop shell for Santiago de Compostela in Spain, keys for Saint Peter in Rome and a cross or palm leaf for Jerusalem. For some the motivation would have been entirely religious, but for many others it was far more basic and earthly - the sick hoping saintly relics would cure their bodily ills, criminals forced to take the long haul as a custodial sentence and the rest banking on enhanced pilgrim credibility and status when they got back home.

St. Helena ... Empress, Saint and first recorded Christian pilgrim to Rome

Helena was a humble innkeeper's daughter from Bithyna. It was said that as a girl, she had been one of the supplementary amenities of her father's establishment, regularly available to clients, at an extra charge. Helena married Constantius and was the mother of Emperor Constantine I (born 274) but she was abandoned by her husband so that he could marry Emperor Maximus' adopted stepdaughter, Theodora. Without any ties, Helena was able to embark upon a pilgrimage to Jerusalem in 324 and arrived in Rome with her son Constantine in 326. Later, aged 70, she made another pilgrimage to tour principal shrines in the Holy Land and is said to have unearthed the True Cross, which she sent back to Rome. Her discovery was endorsed by the Emperor who built the Church of the Holy Sepulchre to house it. The length of her stay in the Holy Land is unknown but she probably died there.

Today's Pilgrim

"To set out on a pilgrimage is to throw down a challenge to everyday life."

Phil Cousineau - the Art of Pilgrimage

The pilgrimage is experiencing a renaissance. In 1986, just 2,491 pilgrims collected their Compostela certificate in Santiago, but by 2006 these figures had passed the 100,000 mark. Today's pilgrimage attracts people of all ages, all beliefs and a variety of motivations. Nevertheless, a frequently stated emotion is the need to stand back and take time to reflect on their own lives and the lives of those around them. Some pilgrims will travel on foot, others will opt for bicycles, horses or even cars, but ultimately, irrespective of the mode of transport or motivation, everyone will find themselves changed by the experience, including the people living along the route who will profit from the cross-cultural exchange and the pilgrim trade. Travelling as a Pilgrim can only ever be at the speed your own body and mental attitude will allow, which may initially seem like a restriction, but even the most cynical and reluctant newcomer will quickly realize that this is in fact a first step on the road to freedom. There will be days when you wonder why the hell you are there, but rest assured, this is only a temporary condition and you will find the answer in the people you meet and the memories you take away.

In 2006, Romano Prodi (in his role as Italian prime minister) vowed to restore the Via Francigena to its former glory. A 7 million Euro budget for ancient roads was set aside to restore the Francigena in Italy and in 2007, Romano Prodi held a ceremony to unveil the first in a series of over 1,500 signs due to be posted along the route. Since then the work has continued and the route has been redefined, with the aim to install signs every 300 metres. In preparation for this 2009 edition of the LightFoot Guide from the Summit of the Great St Bernard Pass to Rome, the authors have physically examined the route between Ivrea and the overall conclusions are as follows:

The Route

The official route is a great improvement over all previous routes and benefits significantly from being recommended and owned by the local communities or local branches of hiking groups such as the CAI (Club Alpino Italiano).

The route succeeds in continuing to reduce the amount of the journey needed on the busy SS and SP roads and where this is unavoidable excellent and very specific recommendations have been made to the ministry and the communities for additional safety measures.

Some route improvements come at the cost of additional distance and sometimes more strenuous hiking. In this 2009 edition the authors have exclusively adopted the official route where there is clear advantage for all groups (hikers, bikers and horse-riders). But where the official route too challenging for one or more group, alternatives are offered.

Signs

The signing activity is being undertaken at a community level and the examples seen by your LightFoot guide authors were excellent. However at this time a number of communities have yet to undertake the work and so the signs can stop abruptly at a community frontier.

The outstanding work is due to be completed by summer of 2009, but this will depend on local cooperation.

Pilgrims should not plan to depend on the signs alone as there is already evidence of erosion/vandalism of installed signs. Ministry signs are the default design, but the signing standards do vary from community to community. For example in the Aosta valley the existing yellow footpath signs are supplemented with a pilgrim logo, while in the area around Fidenza the community uses a small format sign with the pilgrim and stars of Europe. From Aulla to Luni the red and white CAI signs are dominant.

This book traces the Via Francigena from Besançon to Vercelli. You will find an introductory section followed by16 chapters, each of which covers a segment of the route.

Each chapter contains:

A route summary
A cultural and historical overview of the region
Detailed Instructions
Map
Altitude profile

Layout

The entire distance has been divided into manageable sections of approximately 28 kilometres, but accommodation (where it exists) is listed for the entire length of the section so that is up to you and your body where you decide to stop.

Instructions

The entire route has been GPS traced and logged using way point co-ordinates. On this basis, it should be possible to navigate the route using only the written instructions, though a map is provided for additional support and general orientation. Use of a compass is recommended.

Each instruction sheet provides:

Detailed directions corresponding to GPS way point numbers on the map
Verification Point - additional verification of current position
Distance (in metres) between each way point

Each map provides:

A north/south visual representation of the route with way point numbers
Altitude Profile for the section
Icons indicating places to stay, monuments etc. (see Map symbols)
Relevant signs to look out for along the route
Map reference number/s for the section

Accommodation Listings:

Accomodation prices are based on one double room per night - accurate at the time of entry, but subject to change. For simplicity, the listing is divided into 3 price bands:

B1 0-20 € B2 21-50 € B3 51-70 €

In general there are no listings above 70£/€ per night, unless nothing else is available in the area. Prices may or may not include breakfast and some establishments charge a tariff for dogs. In general, dogs are not welcome in Youth or Religious Hostels. Similarly, the general rule for accommodation in Religious Houses is that reservations must be made 24 hours ahead of arrival. The title 'Parish Accommodation' is used where it is in a church hall with minimal facilities. At the end of this section you will also find details of churches and religious organisations either in or near towns along the route.

Look out for the PR - Pilgrim Recommended - in front of listings

LightFoot Tracker

The Via Francigena has the benefit and also the drawback of being less well developed than the Saint James Way. The sense of adventure of travelling a less well developed way and the escape from commercialism is very positive, however the smaller numbers also reduce the opportunity of those wonderful meetings with pilgrims from other backgrounds, with whom you are able to share experiences and often make new friendships.

Today, it is possible that you could follow one day behind or ahead of another group and still meet no other pilgrim on the entire journey. Or spend a night in the same town as another group and be unaware of their existence. We feel that these are lost opportunities and would like to let you know of some work we are doing to develop a few computer tools to help improve this situation.

1. A planning program that will enable you to quickly calculate your likely stop-over points and arrival dates based on your preferred rate of progress, departure date and rest or sight-seeing stops.

2. The facility to publish your plan and appropriate contact details on the internet in a visual form - probably using google earth.

3. The facility to review the plans of others and spot possible cross-over points - again using google earth facilities - giving you the opportunity to schedule a meeting or even find travel partners.

4. A simple process to record your progress along the route and display the progress to others to allow ad hoc meetings.

5. A database of completed journeys with details of age, pack-weight and rate of progress, that can be used to advise future pilgrims.

As a further stage we would like to bring our accommodation data into this environment to facilitate, budgeting and advance booking.

We will keep registered purchasers of the books up to date with progress on these developments through www.pilgrimagepublications.com and our periodic newsletter. We would also welcome your ideas for related functions.

Food, drink and a place to collapse at the end of the day

If you have 'done' the St James Way (pilgrimage equivalent of the M25) and expect the same level of support in terms of cheap accommodation and foraging, then think again. Even along its most well known sections in Italy, the Via Francigena attracts only a fraction of the number of pilgrims and has the corresponding number of pilgrim hostels - very few. In brief, your journey will be much more expensive, unless you plan to live on hedgerow fruits and camp *au sauvage* every night. Correspondingly, do not expect to meet cohorts of pilgrims as you can on the St James Way. This is an undeveloped route, which brings its own advantages, but it's isolation is an aspect everyone needs to be aware of before starting out.

The French section is a great experience, not to be missed, but challening in terms of the practicalities pilgrim travel. Being the European Union's leading agricultural producer means that a huge percentage of its land is given over to farming, which in some areas will amount to endless, depressing and environmentally damaging cereal deserts. In parallel, France is also the most visited country in the world (over 75 million visitors a year), which, if our experience is anything to go by, also amounts to a lot of hungry and homeless tourists. Travelling through northern France on foot is a lesson in survival and ingenuity. The map may tell you there is a village only a few kilometres ahead, but be warned, those little squares indicating houses are just that, houses. France has sold its soul to the car and hyper market, with the result that you will be lucky to find a café or shop in anything smaller than a town. And even if you do, you can bet your bottom Euro that it will be closed for lunch or *en vacance*. In short, the watch-word is assume the worst, carry food for the day, stop where you know you can replenish your supplies and always phone ahead to ensure that the place you have chosen to stay in still exists, is open and has a room available for the night you need it. But, having given you a bleak view of France, it is also important to stress that the French are extremely welcoming and a knock on the door of the local priest or *Mairie* will usually end in a solution. We have done our best to help you by indicating places where you can eat and buy supplies, but this is by no means a comprehensive list and only a fall-back option for those days when your own personal planning has gone awry. In other words - and here comes the metaphorical small print - Don't Blame Us when you are hungry and homeless in France! The Swiss section is relatively simple in terms of accommodation and supplies. Most small towns have at least one shop and a place to stay is never far away. The only, possibly unpleasant change, will be in the terrain, which quite suddenly becomes vertical and rough on the Great St Bernard Pass. Cyclists and walkers will find it tough, but negotiable. Horse-riders are advised to prepare thoroughly, check the route for potential hazards and ensure that their horses are fit. We have tried to provide sufficient information, but ultimately only you can know your horse and what he/she is capable of.

Cyclists - To Road or Off-road

Quite simply if you are a *Roadie* our route is not for you, though of course it is possible to follow an approximate version of the Via Francigena by using road maps. Off-road bikers can go just about anywhere a walker or horse can, but there are occasions when the pain/pleasure ratio makes other options preferable and sensible. We have ridden both horses and bikes the length of the route and know the disadvantages and pleasures of each, so it is with this experience in mind that we offer alternatives where we think it necessary. Of course ultimately these are only guidelines and everyone has to make their own choice. When making yours, bear in mind that we are both on the wrong side of 40, do not enjoy extreme sports and had never ridden a bike further than the shops before setting off for Rome (a state to which this writer is quite happy to return).

About Travel

In terms of what kind of bikes you should use, clearly something fairly robust with an impressive range of gears to conquer those all too numerous hills is a minimum. We bought a couple of sturdy, but not very expensive versions, which survived and still look as if they could do another trip without too much trouble, but there are undoubtedly others available that would have been easier to use in adversity.

Horses and Riders - to Go or not to Go

Make no mistake, riding along the Via Francigena is going to be tough and full of unexpected challenges. For people travelling without back-up, finding fodder and a place to stay will be the greatest challenge, but also the greatest pleasure when it goes well. Turning up in a village or town with a horse and a Don Quixote air can have the most amazing, invariably positive, consequences. Equestrian establishments are listed when they are within a reasonable distance of the route (we have never been turned away), as are the few *chambre d'hôte* proprietors prepared to accommodate horses, but essentially pilgrim riders must use their initiative and be prepared to ask for help. As for farriers and vets, they are listed along the route, but of course we cannot guarantee their competence or availability.

Signs Are Not Always What They Seem To Be

It is a feature of French roads that the responsibility for their maintenance can be transferred between State and Commune. Presumably this has something to do with finance, but the most obvious change is in the number, which can be confusing for the uninitiated, but is basically very simple. *Route Nationale* or 'N' roads can become Minor roads, classed as 'D' roads, which means dropping the N, adding a D and then a number - for example the N32 is now the D1032. These changes are not restricted to standard road signs, but can also appear within the Via Francigena network too - a potentially disorientating factor. In some cases this may be because a commune has made efforts to map the route according to local boundaries and enthusiasms - a degree of involvement everyone should applaud, unless it happens after the production of the guide book and without informing the guide writers. Hence the importance of pilgrim feedback to keep the information as current as possible. Users of the guide may also notice that, on occasion, pilgrims are advised to ignore a Via Francigena sign. This is never an easy decision, but it is always based on bitter experience (usually after hours of trudging along a track that has either lapsed into disuse, or has been ploughed into oblivion by a farmer). Again, pilgrim feedback is fundamental for the accurate maintenance of the information in this guide.

If you have bought this book, presumably you have chosen to try the English/French section and maybe even the whole route, in which case - good on you. As already mentioned, the French section is less well signed and less well known than its Italian equivalent, but it is a unique cross-section through France's landscape, history and culture and an experience impossible to achieve in any other way.

Behaviour on the Road - preserve our heritage

Following pilgrim routes on foot, bicycle or horse is potentially the most eco-friendly form of travel possible. It can also benefit the local economy so that pilgrim tourists are always welcome, but this will only be the case if a few very simple rules are followed. Some sections of popular pilgrim routes are ruined by pilgrim detritus: plastic bottles, bags, tissues, sanitary towels, toilet paper ... an unsightly mess that is also a great deal more serious for the environment and wildlife. Everyone is responsible for the maintenance of these historic routes and should dispose of their rubbish in the appropriate way. Horse riders face an additional responsibility in this respect, because horses/donkeys can destroy turf and decimate gardens in seconds. Large piles of steaming, fly-clustered manure outside a restaurant are not good for trade and people do not like having metal shod hooves on their open-toed sandals. Whether you are walking, cycling or riding, please think about these points when you are travelling

Health and Safety

The most general and obvious health and safety tips apply to everyone; walker, cyclist or rider. This route should present no serious problems even to a beginner, provided you follow a few simple rules.

Don't take unnecessary risks by tackling overly long or difficult routes.

Know where you are or have a map and the ability to read it.

On longer walks, be aware of "escape routes" in case you need to cut your walk short.

Make sure you have plenty to eat and drink and are adequately dressed for the length of time you'll be out.

Check the forecast before you set out and keep an eye on the sky. Rain, mist or fog and cold are the obvious hazards.

The route recommended by this guide avoids roads wherever possible, but you will encounter some. In these situations, use the pavement if there is one and safe crossings wherever possible.

Walkers

Walking up hills increases the work load and energy cost considerably; even walking down again uses more energy than walking on the flat. Walking downhill can also make you sore if you're unaccustomed to it, because it uses muscles as shock absorbers. Plan rest days to allow your muscles and feet to recover. There is some controversy over how to treat blisters when they do occur. Some walkers prefer to burst the blister carefully and immediately apply a sterile dressing. Others argue this runs the risk of infection and instead recommend gel-filled blister plasters. Either way, injuries and blisters are miserable and if serious enough can put an end to your plan, so avoidance is the best tactic.

Rucksack: the general principle should be to carry only what you need and no more. This route will not take you far away from civilization and on most days shops, hotels and hostels will be easily accessible, though riders with horses may have to plan further ahead. In all cases your rucksack should be large enough to take a tent and sleeping bag, if only as a fallback measure if things go awry.

Footwear: You will only need a pair of light walking boots, because you will not encounter any severe climbs (in France at least), but you should take a pair of comfortable sandals or trainers to give your feet a break at the end of the day.

Clothing: waterproofs are a must, along with a fleece for the cooler evenings. Plan according to the time of year that you are travelling, but never rely on the weather. It will always do the unexpected.

Cyclists

The reality of long distance unsupported cycling trips is that you have to carry everything with you, and you have to wash clothes every night so Lycra is a good option. If you are

thinking of cycling, you probably have your own bicycle already and providing it is a reasonable quality mountain bike, it will be adequate. Try to minimise the weight you are carrying. The more weight the greater the energy output required to carry it. There is a wide variety of racks available to support your panniers, but choose one of solid construction because it will take a lot of punishment. The mountings and securing nuts must be checked daily.
Injuries:The most common causes of cycling-related injuries are incorrect riding posture, such as putting too much weight on the hands and riding with straight elbows. Knee injury is generally due to overuse and occurs when a cyclist is doing too much, too fast. Once you've crested the hill, avoid the temptation to coast down the other side. Pedal a little bit to reduce the risk of lactic acid build-up in your leg muscles.

Horses and Riders

Don't even consider going on the Via Francigena with your horse or donkey before you have ensured that:

He/she is one hundred percent traffic proof
He/she is familiar with crowds and generally noisy places
He/she can be tethered for a full night
He/she can deal with a variety of different feeds.

Equipment: The equipment you take will be governed by two factors: importance and weight - two priorities you must literally weigh up before leaving. There are probably as many opinions as riders on the best equipment to be used, so we will not enter that particular minefield here. Use the tack that you know your horse can tolerate for extended distances without suffering from galls and use a saddle pad that will distribute the weight as much as possible. Another point to note is that you will meet difficult terrain, so make sure all of your equipment will stay in place on both steep climbs and descents. Be sure to test it all before you leave. Despite all of your best endeavours your equipment will be lost, stolen or worn out by the time you return home, so be sure that what you take you are happy to lose. If you want to use a pack pony, consult the professionals and make sure you test your gear and your pony thoroughly before you go. Don't carry a huge veterinary kit. A can of antiseptic spray, an anti-inflammatory gel or something similar, and (if you are allowed to) a course of antibiotics, is ample. The Via Francigena is not the North Pole and you can find vets and chemists along the route without any difficulty.
Absolutely indispensable:

Canvas water buckets

Plastic gloves and plastic bags to pick up the inevitable equine accident. Horse riders have as much responsibility for the behaviour of their horses as do dog owners for their dogs.

We recommend leather chaps, a waterproof cape and a broad brimmed hat.

So there you have it, the few words of wisdom we have to offer. Pilgrim feedback is fundamental for the accurate maintenance of the information in this guide, so please let us know where the route has changed, our information is incorrect or you can add to what we have. And remember, you are not doing this for us, but for all the pilgrims who will follow in your footsteps.

Currency: Euro. **Standard banking Hours:** Monday-Friday 09.30-12.00 and 14.00-16.00. Closed on Sundays and usually Monday, with half day opening on Saturday morning

Post Offices (La Poste): Standard opening hours Mon - Fri - 09.30-12.00 and 14.00-17.00. Half day opening on Saturday morning.

You can make domestic and international **phone calls** from any public telephone box and can receive calls where there is a new logo of a ringing bell.

Emergencies - 112 will give you access to the following services: Fire, Police, Ambulance, Coastguard, Mountain rescue or Cave rescue. This is free and can be dialled from any telephone (including mobile phones).

Basic Business Hours - 08.00-12.00 and 14.00-18.00. Almost everything in France - shops, museums, tourist offices etc. - closes for two hours at midday. Food shops often don't reopen until half way through the afternoon, but close at 19.30 or 20.00. The standard closing days are Sunday and Monday in small towns, but you will find that many large supermarkets are now staying open throughout the day.

All EU citizens are eligible for free **health care** if they have the correct documentation. The UK's NHS care includes free visits to the local doctor, and paying a standard charge for prescriptions and dental treatment.

In France, the best way of **eating** breakfast is in a bar or café, at a fraction of the cost charged by most hotels. Expect a croissant or some bread with coffee or hot chocolate. At lunchtime and sometimes in the evenings you'll find most cafés and restaurants offering a *plat du jour*, which is by far the cheapest alternative if you don't fancy cooking yourself.

In country areas, in addition to standard hotels, you will come across ***chambre d'hôtes*** and ***ferme auberge***, bed and breakfast accommodation in someone's house or farm. These are rarely an especially cheap option, usually costing the equivalent of a two star hotel.

Youth hostels (***auberges de jeunesse***) are great for travellers on a budget. They are often beautifully sited and they allow you to cut costs by preparing your own food in their kitchens or eating in cheap canteens. The majority will require that you are a member of the International Youth Hostel Federation.
Gites d'étape are basic but do not require membership and provide bunk beds with primitive kitchen and washing facilities at a reasonable price.

Campsites in France are nearly always clean and have plenty of hot water. On the coast there are superior categories of campsite where you will pay prices similar to those of a hotel for the facilities -bars, restaurants and usually elaborate swimming pools too. For horses, it is useful to know that campsite owners often allow horses to be tethered at the edge of the site.

About the Basics in Switzerland

Currency: **Swiss Franc CHF**. Standard banking Hours: 08:30–16:30 (Mon–Fri). Closed on Sundays

Swiss Post Standard Opening Hours: 07.30-1200 and 13.45-18.30 Monday to Friday.Mon - Fri - 09.30-12.00 and 14.00-17.00. Half day opening on Saturday morning.

Some **phone** booths still accept coins, but they are not easy to find. If you're planning to use a public phone, it is recommended that you buy a telephone card.

Phone cards can be bought for CHF 5, 10, 20 or 50. Cards for CHF 20 or 50 have a band on each side of the card. In most public telephone boxes it is also possible to be rung back. If so, you will find a sign with the phone's number displayed on it. Emergencies - If you don't know where to call, dial the police on 117 who will tell you where to call or directly connect you. If you need ambulance, dial 144.

Basic Business Hours Monday, Tuesday, Wednesday, Friday 9 a.m. - 6:30 p.m. Shops in smaller towns and villages may close on Monday (either morning or all day). Thursday 9 a.m. - 8 or 9 p.m. (mainly in larger cities and towns). Saturday 9 a.m. - 4 p.m. Sunday and holidays closed (except for bakeries, which may be open in the morning).

Health care - Switzerland has concluded agreements with the EU states as well as the EFTA states Iceland and Norway, which provide for a so-called mutual benefits assistance. Citizens living outside these countries must arrange personal health insurance.

Swiss cuisine draws heavily on its influences from its French, Italian and German neighbours. In the German-speaking region, the food takes its influence from the climatic and geographic conditions of the area and features soup and heavier kinds of food. There are also some good wines worth investigating, but watch out - nothing in Switzerland is cheap.

Swiss hotels are very similiar to the French,in terms of the types available. In addition to standard hotels, you will also find **chambre d'hotes, ferme auberge** and **bed and breakfast** accommodation in someone's house or farm. Youth hostels are a good, cheap option, but unfortunately there are not many on the Via Francigena route.

As you would probably expect, Swiss **campsites** are well equipped and provide just about everything the average camper will need. Price and location are the only possible drawbacks.

Currency: **Euro**. Standard banking Hours: 08.30–13.30 and 14.30-16.00, Monday to Friday. Closed on Sundays.

Post Offices - Standard Opening Hours: 08.30-19.30 and 13.45-18.30, Monday to Friday. Branches in smaller towns and villages close for an hour, 13.00-14.00.

Phone booths that still accept coins are hard find. If you're planning to use a public phone purchase of a telephone card is recommended.
Numbers beginning with 800 are free.
170 - English-speaking operator.
176 - International Directory Enquires.
12 - Telephone Directory Assistance Number
112 - *Carabinieri* (national-level police who also perform military police duties)
113 - Emergency Police Help Number (also ambulance and fire)
115 - Fire Department
116 - A.C.I. (Italian Automobile Club) road assistance.
118 - Medical Emergencies
Note: Italian telephone numbers can include 4, 5, 6, 7, or even 8 digits, so don't automatically assume you have the wrong number if it looks strange. Since December 1998, calls to land lines in most cities, but not all, and all other points in Italy must include a leading '0' regardless of whether the call originates within or outside of Italy. However, the leading '0' is not required with mobile phones. The '0' is shown as (0) throughout the guide, in order to draw your attention to this potential confusion.

Basic Business Hours 08.00-13.00 and 16.00-19.00, Monday to Friday. Shops in smaller towns may close on Saturday afternoons and Monday mornings.

Visting **churches and religious sites**. Most churches are open in the early morning for Mass and close around noon, opening up again at 16.00 and closing at 19.00 or 20.00. In some remote places, churches only open for early morning and evening services. Opening hours for museums are generally Tuesday to Saturday, 09.00 to 19.00 with a midday break.

All EU citizens are eligible for free **health care** in Italy, if they have the correct documentation. Non EU Citizens must arrange personal health insurance.

Traditionally **Italian food** consists of lunch (*pranzo*) and dinner (*cena*) starting with *antipasto* (literally before the meal), a course consisting of cold meats, seafood and vegetables. The next course, *primo*, involves soup, risotto or pasta, followed by *secondo* - the meat or fish course, usually served alone. Vegetables - *contorni* - are ordered and served separately.
Pizza is now a worldwide phenomenon, but Italy remains the best place to eat it.
Italian ice cream (*gelato*) is justifiably famous and available in every conceivable flavour.

Public Holidays - August, particularly during the weeks either side of *Ferragosto* (August 15) is a difficult time for travellers, because many towns are deserted, with shops, bars, hotels and restaurants shut.

Italian **hotels** fall into a number of categories, though the difference between each is gradually decreasing.
Locanda - historically the most basic option, but now tending to charge more for 'traditional' facilities.
Pensione, albergo or hotel - prices vary greatly between tourist hotspots and rural areas. Expect an additional charge for breakfast.
Hostels usually charge 15€. Virtually all hostels (excepting Religious Hostels) are members of the International Youth Hostel Association and you'll need to be a member.
Agritourismo - basically an upmarket B&B in a rural area and usually a working farm (see Travel tips for more information)
Camping in Italy is popular and the sites are generally well equipped.

About General French Vocabulary

ENGLISH	FRENCH	ENGLISH	FRENCH
Sunday	dimanche	one	un
Monday	lundi	two	deux
Tuesday	mardi	three	trois
Wednesday	mercredi	four	quatre
Thursday	jeudi	five	cinq
Friday	vendredi	six	six
Saturday	samedi	seven	sept
January	janvier	eight	huit
February	février	nine	neuf
March	mars	ten	dix
April	avril	eleven	onze
May	mai	twelve	douze
June	juin	thirteen	treize
July	juillet	fourteen	quatorze
August	août	fifteen	quinze
September	septembre	sixteen	seize
October	octobre	seventeen	dix-sept
November	novembre	eighteen	dix-huit
December	décembre	nineteen	dix-neuf
today	aujourd'hui	twenty	vingt
yesterday	hier	thirty	trente
tomorrow	demain	forty	quarante
in the morning	le matin	fifty	cinquante
in the afternoon	l'après-midi	sixty	soixante
in the evening	le soir	seventy	soixante-dix
now	maintenant	seventy-five	soixante-quinze
later	plus tard	eighty	quatre-vingts
at midday	à midi	ninety	quatre-vingt-dix
at one o'clock	à une heure	one hundred	cent
bus	autobus, bus, car	on the other side of	à l'autre côte de
bus stop	arrêt	on the corner of	à l'angle de
bus station	gare routière	next to	à côte de
car	voiture	behind	derrière
train station	gare	in front of	devant
what time does it arrive/leave?	il arrive/part à quelle heure?	before	avant
how many kilometres	combien de kilomètres?	after	aprés
how many hours	combien d'heures?	under	sous
on foot	à pied	to cross	traverser
the road to	la route à	where?	ou?
near	prés/pas loin	when?	quand?
far	loin	how many/much?	combien?
left	à gauche	why?	pourquoi?
right	à droite	at what time?	a quelle heure?
straight on	tout droit	a room for one/two person/people	une chambre pour une/deux personnes

Cycling

ENGLISH	FRENCH	ENGLISH	FRENCH
to adjust	ajuster	to lower	baisser
axle	l'axe	mudguard	le garde-boue
ball bearing	le roulement à billes	pannier	le panier
battery	la pile	pedal	la pédale
bent	tordu	pump	la pompe
bicycle	le vélo	puncture	la crevaison
brake cable	le câble	to raise	relever
brakes	les freins	to repair	réparer
broken	cassé	saddle	la selle
bulb	l'ampoule	to screw	visser
chain	la chaine	spanner	la clef
to deflate	dégonfler	spoke	le rayon
frame	le cadre	to straighten	redresser
gears	les vitesses	stuck	coincé
grease	la graisse	tight	serré
handlebars	le guidon	toe clips	les cale-pieds
to inflate	gonfler	tyre	pneu
inner tube	la chambre à air	wheel	la roue

Equine

ENGLISH	FRENCH	ENGLISH	FRENCH
stud (to put in horse shoe)	un crampon	stirrup	etrier
mane	la crinière	saddle pad	tapis de selle
tail	la queue	brush	brosse
horse	cheval	hoof-picks	cure-pieds
mare	jument	horse shoe	fer
foal	poulain	helmet	bombe
gelding	hongre	hat	chapeau
stallion	entier / etalon	gloves	gants
head	tête	boots	bottes
eyes	yeux	walk	pas
ears	oreilles	trot	trot
nostril	naseau	canter	galop
withers	garrot	saddle	selle
croup (rear)	croupe	girth	sangle
neck	encolure	bridle	bride
mane	crinière	rope	longe
legs	jambes	to unsaddle	desseller
hoof	sabot	to girth	sangler
tack	harnachement (général)	to loosen the girth	dessangler
lame	boiter	to shorten	raccourcir

About General German Vocabulary

ENGLISH	GERMAN	ENGLISH	GERMAN
Sunday	Sonntag	one	ein
Monday	Montag	two	zwei
Tuesday	Dienstag	three	drei
Wednesday	Mittwoch	four	vier
Thursday	Donnerstag	five	fünf
Friday	Freitag	six	sechs
Saturday	Samstag	seven	sieben
January	Januar	eight	acht
February	Februar	nine	neun
March	März	ten	zehn
April	April	eleven	elf
May	Mai	twelve	zwölf
June	Juni	thirteen	dreizehn
July	Juli	fourteen	vierzehn
August	August	fifteen	fünfzehn
September	September	sixteen	sechzehn
October	Oktober	seventeen	siebzehn
November	November	eighteen	achtzehn
December	Dezember	nineteen	neunzehn
today	heute	twenty	zwanzig
yesterday	gestern	thirty	dreißig
tomorrow	morgen	forty	vierzig
in the morning	am Morgen	fifty	fünfzig
in the afternoon	am Nachmittag	sixty	sechzig
in the evening	am Abend	seventy	siebzig
now	jetzt	seventy-five	fünfundsiebzig
later	später	eighty	achtzig
at midday	am Mittag	ninety	neunzig
at one o'clock	um ein Uhr	one hundred	hundert
bus	Bus	on the other side	auf der anderen Seite
bus station	Busbahnhof	next to	nebenan/ daneben
car	Auto	behind	hinten
train station	Bahnhof	in front of	vor
how many kilometres	wie viele Kilometer	after	nach
how many hours	wie vielen Stunden	under	unter
on foot	zu Fuß	to cross over	kreuzen
the road to	die Strasse nach	where?	wo?
near	nah	when?	wann?
far	weit	how ?	wie?
left	links	why?	warum?
right	rechts	at what time?	um welche Zeit?
straight on	gerade aus	a room for one/two person/people	ein Zimmer für eine Person/ zwei Personen

Cycling

ENGLISH	GERMAN	ENGLISH	GERMAN
to adjust	einstellen/anpassen	to lower	senken
axle	Achsel	mudguard	Schutzblech
battery	Batterie	pedal	Pedal
bent	gebogen	pump	Pumpe
bicycle	Fahrrad	puncture	Reifenpanne
bottom bracket	untere Schutzklammer	rack	Rahmengestell
brake cable	Bremskabel	to raise	anheben/erhöhen
brakes	Bremse	repair	reparatur
broken	gebrochen	saddle	Sattel
bulb	Glühbirne	screw	Schraube
chain	Kette	spanner	Schraubenschlüssel
to deflate	entleeren/luft ablassen	spoke	Radspeiche
frame	Rahmen	to straighten	geraderichten/ ausrichten
gears	Gänge	stuck	festgeklemmt/ eingeklemmt
to be stuck	Steckenbleiben	wheel	Rad
grease	Fett	tight	fest/dicht/straff
handlebars	Lenkstangen	toe clips	Pedalhacken
to inflate	aufblasen	tyre	Reifen

Equine

ENGLISH	GERMAN	ENGLISH	GERMAN
stallion	Hengst	gloves	Handschuhe
head	Kopf	boots	Stiefel
eyes	augen	to walk	gehen/laufen
a walk	spaziergang/ wanderung	walk of a horse/gait	gangart/gang/schritt
ear	Ohr	to canter	kantern
trot	traben	trot	trab
gallop	galoppieren	saddle	Sattel
girth	Gurt	nostril (horse)	nüster
hoof	Huf	Bridle	zaunzeug
neck	Hals	Rope	seil
withers	Widerrist	to unsaddle	absatteln
croup (rear)	Kruppe	to girth	gurteinfassen
to loosen the girth	gurteinfassung lösen	Leg	bein

ENGLISH	ITALIAN	ENGLISH	ITALIAN
Sunday	Domenica	one	uno
Monday	Lunedi	two	due
Tuesday	Martedi	three	tre
Wednesday	Mercoledi	four	quattro
Thursday	Giovedi	five	cinque
Friday	Venerdi	six	sei
Saturday	Sabato	seven	sette
January	Gennaio	eight	otto
February	Febbraio	nine	nove
March	Marzo	ten	dieci
April	Aprile	eleven	undici
May	Maggio	twelve	dodici
June	Giugno	thirteen	tredici
July	Luglio	fourteen	quattordici
August	Agosto	fifteen	quindici
September	Septembre	sixteen	sedici
October	Octobre	seventeen	diciassette
November	Novembre	eighteen	diciotto
December	Dicembre	nineteen	diciannove
today	oggi	twenty	venti
yesterday	ieri	thirty	trenta
tomorrow	domani	forty	quaranta
in the morning	alla mattina	fifty	cinquanta
in the afternoon	nel pomeriggio	sixty	sessanta
in the evening	nella sera	seventy	settanta
now	ora	eighty	ottanta
later	piu successivamente	ninety	novanta
at midday	al mezzogiorno	one hundred	cento
at one o'clock	un in punto	on the other side of	dall'altro
bus	vettura	on the corner of	sul angolo di
bus stop	arresto di bus	next to	vicino a
bus station	autostazione	behind	dietro
car	automobile	in front of	davanti
train station	stazione di treno	before	prima
what time does it arrive/leave?	quando arriva/va?	after	dopo
how many kilometres	quanti chilometri?	under	sotto
how many hours	quante ora?	to cross	alla traversa sopra
on foot	à piedi	where?	dove?
the road to	la strada a	when?	quando?
near	vicino	how many/much?	quanto?
far	lontano	why?	perche?
left	sinistra	at what time?	a quando?
right	destra	a room for one/two person/people	una stanza per una gente/persona due?
straight on	dritto		

Cycling Vocabulary			
ENGLISH	**ITALIAN**	**ENGLISH**	**ITALIAN**
to adjust	regolare	to lower	abbassare
axle	asse	mudguard	parafango
ball bearing	cuscinetto a sfere	pannier	borsa
battery	batteria	pedal	pedale
bent	inclinazione	pump	pompa
bicycle	bicicletta	puncture	foratura
brake cable	cavo freno	to raise	sollevare
brakes	freni	to repair	riparare
broken	rotto	saddle	sellino
bulb	lampadina	to screw	avvitare
chain	catena	spanner	chiave
to deflate	sgonfiare	spoke	raggio
frame	telaio	to straighten	assettare
gears	marce	stuck	bloccato
grease	grasso	tight	stretto
handlebars	manubri	toe clips	fermapiedi
to inflate	gonfiare	tyre	pneumatico
inner tube	camera d'aria	wheel	ruota

Equine Vocabulary			
Farrier	Veterinario	Stirrup	Staffa
Mane	Criniera	Saddle pad	Sella imbottita
Tail	Coda	Brush	Spazzola
Horse	Cavallo	Hoof-picks	Curasnette
Mare	Giumenta	Horse shoe	Stivali da equitazione
Foal	Puledro	Helmet	Elmetto
Gelding	Cavallo castrato	Hat	Cappello
Stallion	Stallone	Gloves	Guanti
Head	Testa	Boots	Stivali
Eyes	Occhi	Walk	Passo
Ears	Orecchie	Canter Trot	Galoppo Trotto
Nostril	Narici	To limp	Zoppicare
Withers	Garrese	Saddle	Sella
Croup (rear)	Groppa	Girth	Sottopancia
Neck	Collo	Bridle	Briglia
Hay	Fieno	Oats	Avena
Legs	Zampe	To unsaddle	Dissellare
Hoof	Zoccolo	To girth	Assicurare la sella
Tack	Bardatura	To loosen the girth	Allentare il sottopancia
Lame	Zoppo	To shorten	Accorciare

About Useful Links

Pilgrim and Travel Sites	
www.Pilgrimstales.com	PILGRIM TALES publishing is passionate about inspiring others with the possibility of discovery, understanding and peace through travel
www.pilgrimstorome.org.uk	Practical information for the pilgrimage to Rome
www.theexpeditioner.com	THE EXPEDITIONER popular travel-themed webzine featuring articles about travel, music and film.
www.euroVia.tv	EUROVIA serves as a platform made by pilgrims, for pilgrims. Everybody is welcome to share their experiences with others, and to contribute their views and opinions. Other pilgrims are always grateful to receive useful tips
www.camminideuropageie.com	An Italian, Spanish, French collaboration
www.culturalroutes.ch	CULTURAL ROUTES OF SWITZERLAND deals with cultural routes in Switzerland and as such has information about the Via Francigena through that country. At time of writing it is in German and French only
www.francigena.eu	EUROPEAN ASSOCIATION webpage. In Italian. Has photos and maps of the route in Italy though they may not have enough detail for walkers
www.giovannicaselli.com/francigena/italy.htm	VIA FRANCIGENA - HIGHWAY TO HEAVEN Website of Giovanni Caselli. In Italian.
www.groups.yahoo.com/group/Viafrancigena/	VIA FRANCIGENA YAHOO DISCUSSION GROUP A lively discussion group with a large amount of useful information.
www.pelgrimswegen.nl	DUTCH ASSOCIATION OF PILGRIMS TO ROME Site in Dutch
www.canterbury.gov.uk	CANTERBURY CITY COUNCIL
www.csj.org.uk	CONFRATERNITY OF ST JAMES providing a wealth of information about the many pilgrim routes to Santiago de Compostela in Spain as well as general guidance and advice to pilgrims. It is well worth visiting if this is your first pilgrimage.
www.sixtina.com	ITALIA SIXTINA French booking service for lodging in convents and monasteries.
www.stjamesirl.com	IRISH SOCIETY OF THE FRIENDS OF ST JAMES The site of the Irish equivalent to the CSJ.
www.francigena-international.org	INTERNATIONAL ASSOCIATION OF VIA FRANCIGENA publishes maps of the route in walking stages as well as route instructions and accommodation lists.

General

French Tourist Board, 178 Piccadilly, London W1J 9AL Tel: 0044 (0)9068 244 123
info.uk@franceguide.com http://uk.franceguide.com

French Youth Hostelling Association, FUAJ - National Centre Office, 27 rue Pajol, 75018 Paris Tel: 0033 (0)1 44 89 87 27

AIG, NATIONAL BOARD, 44, via Cavour - 00184 ROMA Tel: 0039 06 4871152
info@ostellionline.org
AIG, TRAVEL SECTION, 48/50, via Farini - 00184 ROME Tel: 0039 06 48907740
info@ostellionline.org

Swiss Youth Hostels, 14 Schaffhauserstrasse - 8042 ZÜRICH Tel: 0041 (0)44 360 14 14
bookingoffice@youthhostel.ch

IGN Maps http://ign.fr

Swiss maps available from Kümerley+Frey www.swisstravelcenter.ch

Further Reading

Europe's Monastery and Convent Guest Houses	Kevin J. Wright
The Art of Pilgrimage	Phil Cousineau
Have Saddle Will Travel	Don West
The Essential Walker's Journal	Leslie Sansone
Pilgrimage to Rome in the Middle Ages: Continuity and Change (Studies in the History of Medieval Religion)	Debra J. Birch
The Age of Pilgrimage: The Medieval Journey to God	Jonathan Sumption
The Pilgrim's France - A Travel Guide to the Saints	James & Colleen Heater
Along the Templar Trail	Brandon Wilson
Via Francigena - Impressions of a Pilgrimage	Publisher: Eurovia
The Christian's Guide to Rome	S.G.A Luff
Rome: a pilgrim's companion	David Baldwin (Catholic Truth Society, London)
In Search of a Way: two journeys of spiritual discovery	Gerard Hughes
Pilgrim-Diary, Nikulas of Munkathvera: the Road to Rome	Francis P. Magoun

Signs to look out for in Italy

Restaurant

Café

Accommodation

Grocery

Campsite

Tourist Information Office

Railway Station

Equestrian Centre

Monument

Airfield

Major church or other religious building

Parish church

Canal

Railway

River

Motorway or major road

Main road

Minor road

via Francigena - on road

via Francigena - off road

Alternate route - on road

Alternate route - off road

The Route

Besançon
to
Vercelli
453 kilometres

The World is a book, and those who do not travel read only a page.

Saint Augustin

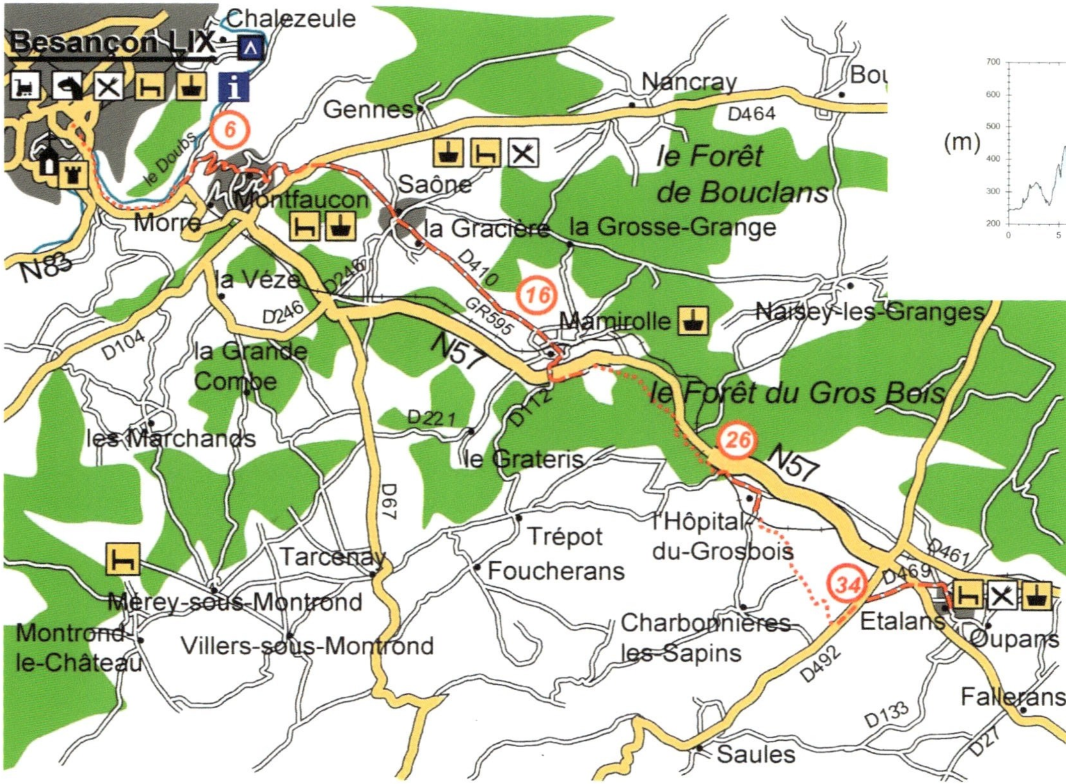

Besançon to Etalans 28.5km

Altitude Profile

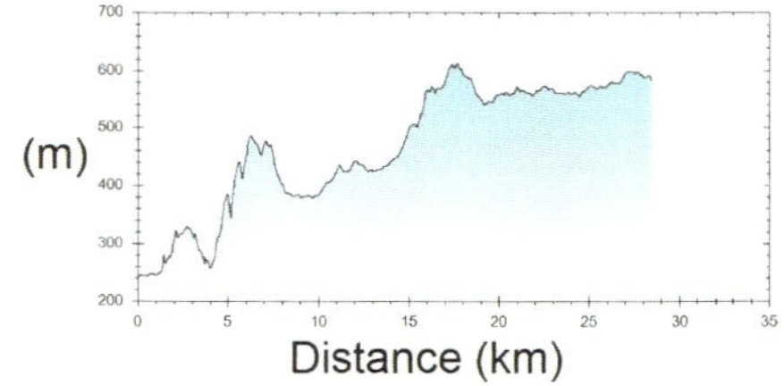

Sign to Look Out For

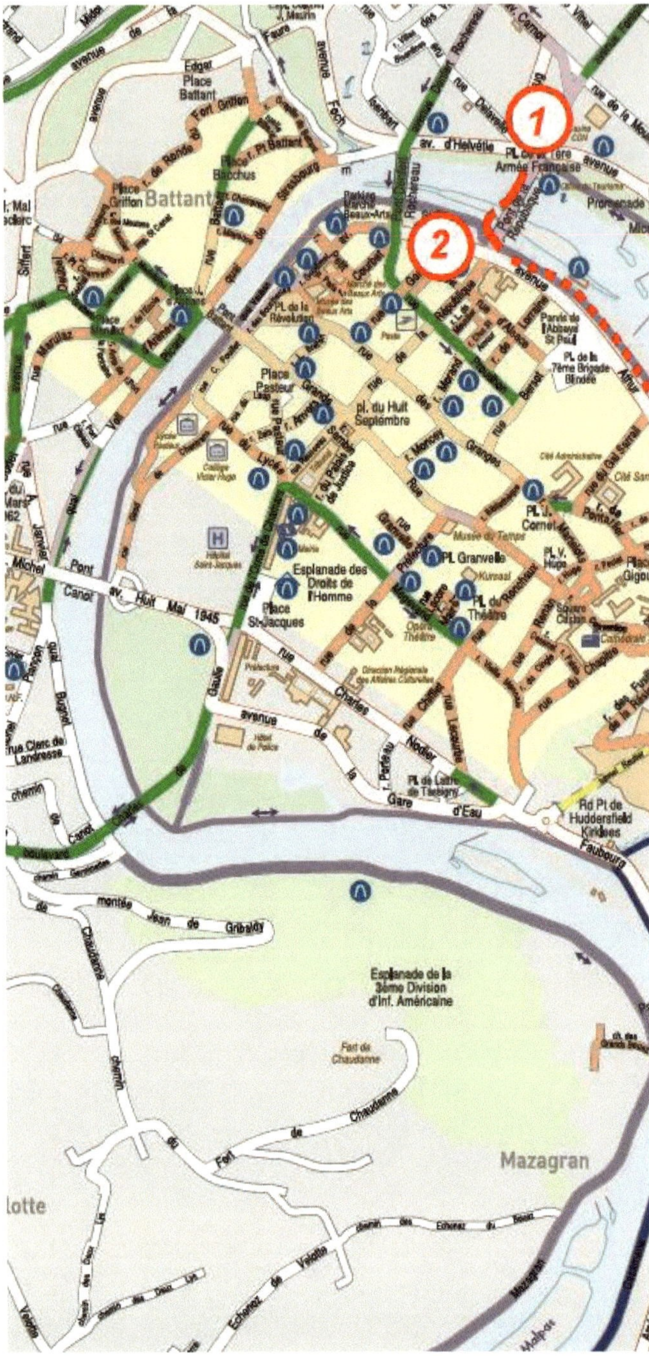
Battant
Place Battant
Place Bacchus
Place Griffon
av. d'Helvétie
PL de la 1ère Armée Française
Promenade
1
2
PL de la Révolution
Place Pasteur
pl. du Huit Septembre
Parvis de l'Abbaye St Paul
PL de la 7ème Brigade Blindée
Cité Administrative
PL J. Cornet
PL V. Hugo
PL Granvelle
PL du Théâtre
Square Castan
Esplanade des Droits de l'Homme
Place St-Jacques
Pont Canot
av. Huit Mai 1945
rue Charles Nodier
Gare d'Eau
PL de Lattre de Tassigny
Rd Pt de Huddersfield Kirklees
montée Jean de Gribaldy
Esplanade de la 3ème Division d'Inf. Américaine
Fort de Chaudanne
Mazagran

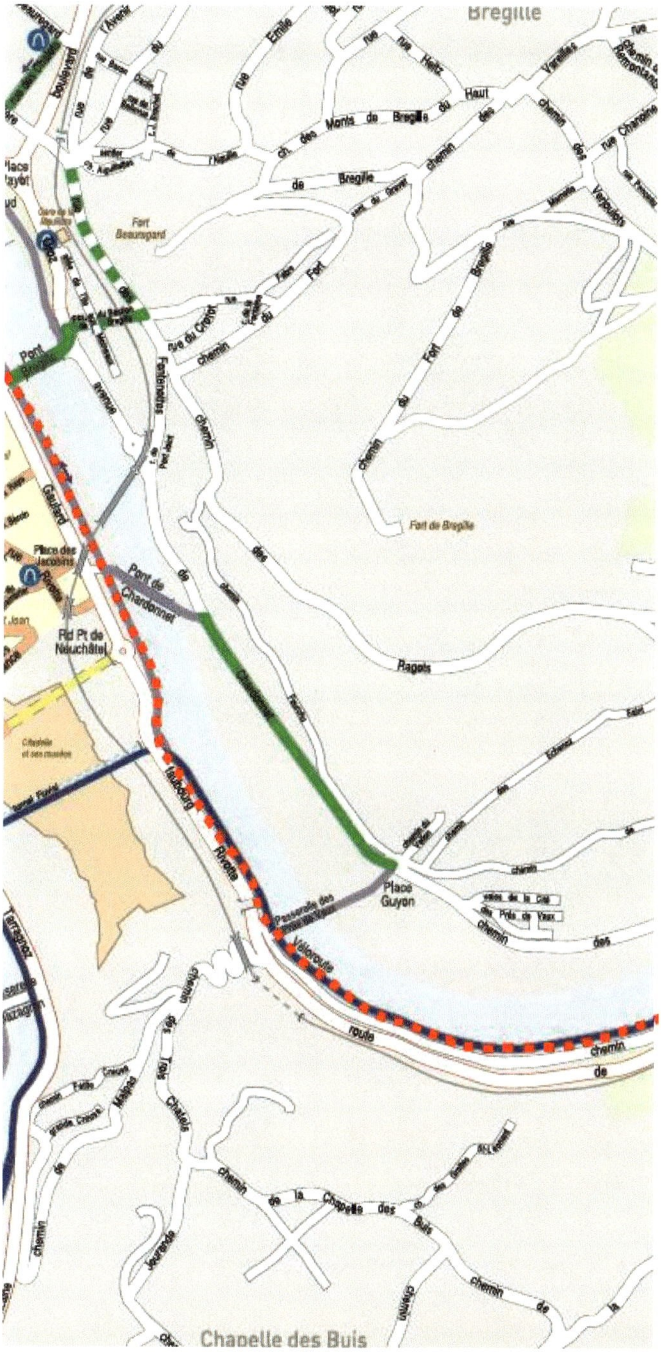
Bregille
Place Guyon
Pont de Chardonnet
Rd Pt de Neuchâtel
Place des Jacobins
Fort de Bregille
Ragots
Rivotte
Gaudard
Véloroute
Chapelle des Buis

Route Summary: the exit from Besançon begins gently alonside the river Doubs. There is a stiff climb on a quiet road from the river into Montfaucon. The road levels and the later parts follow good tracks safely isolated from the busy N57.

Distance from Canterbury: 760km **Distance to Rome:** 1316km

Ascent: 939m **Descent:** 802m

Besançon to Etalans 28.5 km

Way Point N°	Way Point Distance (metres)	Total Distance (kilometres)	Directions	Verification Point	Compass	Altitude (metres)
30.01	0	0.0	Starting from the tourist office take the Pont de la République over the river Doubs		SW	243
30.02	180	0.2	After crossing the river turn left onto the river-side path	Maintain river to the left, passing the Citadel on the right	SE	245
30.03	3500	3.7	Turn right to leave the chemin de Halage		SE	266
30.04	30	3.7	Turn left on chemin de la Malate	Pass beside water works	NE	277
30.05	160	3.9	At fork bear left remaining parallel to the river		N	271
30.06	150	4.0	At next fork bear right on chemin des Vignes	Climb steep hill	E	257
30.07	1600	5.6	At T-junction bear left into village of Montfaucon	rue des Roches	E	480
30.08	160	5.8	At roundabout continue straight ahead	D143	E	485
30.09	300	6.1	Bear left then immediately right on rue de la Vierge	Remain on D143	SE	472
30.10	200	6.3	At divided junction turn sharp left	D146	NE	454
30.11	300	6.6	Turn right direction Saône and Nancray		E	476

Way Point N°	Way Point Distance (metres)	Total Distance (kilometres)	Directions	Verification Point	Compass	Altitude (metres)
30.12	200	6.8	Turn right onto rue de Pérouse		E	471
30.13	900	7.7	At roundabout go straight ahead direction Saône, D104	Roundabout with a large flower pot in the middle	SE	395
30.14	2100	9.8	Proceed straight ahead in the direction of the church	Rue de le Glacière	SE	383
30.15	400	10.2	At crossroads bear left, direction Mamirolle, D410	Tennis courts on left	SE	401
30.16	3400	13.6	At roundabout continue straight ahead		SE	434
30.17	900	14.5	Bear left to take a pedestrian tunnel under the railway		SE	468
30.18	70	14.6	After the railway tunnel continue straight up the hill	Rue de la Gare	SE	474
30.19	300	14.9	Fork right at top of hill on rue de l'Eglise	Fountain directly in front	SW	500
30.20	80	14.9	Bear left left direction Tréspot, D112	Proceed towards church	SW	503
30.21	500	15.4	After crossing the bridge over the busy N57 turn left onto chemin de Mont	GR 595	E	519
30.22	200	15.6	At fork bear left remaining parallel to N57	Telephone tower on right	E	556
30.23	1000	16.6	At fork bear left onto track remain parallel to N57	VF sign	SE	569
30.24	2700	19.3	Stay on the main track and as close to the N57 as possible		SE	540
30.25	1300	20.6	At T-junction turn left onto road	VF sign	NE	556
30.26	190	20.8	At crossroads after level crossing turn right direction l'Hôpital du Grosbois, D387	VF sign	SE	559
30.27	900	21.7	At the church turn right onto rue de la Gare	Direction Charbonnier-les-Sapins	S	560

Way Point N°	Way Point Distance (metres)	Total Distance (kilometres)	Directions	Verification Point	Compass	Altitude (metres)
30.28	100	21.8	Bear left onto rue du Stade		S	560
30.29	400	22.2	Turn left onto track immediately after going over the level crossing	Pass between sports ground and railway	SE	564
30.30	1300	23.5	Track degrades into grass track	Just after passing farm house - le Greffier	S	560
30.31	500	24.0	Track forks bear left		SE	561
30.32	700	24.7	Turn sharp left at the farmyard leaving the farm on your right	Immediately after farm the track emerges onto tarmac	SE	562
30.0033	600	25.3	At road junction turn left	VF sign	NE	567
30.34	800	26.1	Turn right onto D467		E	580
30.35	1200	27.3	Cross straight over N57 on D469, direction Etalans		SE	597
30.36	1200	28.5	Arrive in Etalans centre			581

Hotel/B&B	Price
Les Granges du Liège - 25660 MEREY SOUS MONTROND Tel: 0033 (0)3 81 81 67 90	B2
Mme PASTEUR Sylvie, 14, rue de la vue des Alpes - 25660 MONTFAUCON Tel: 0033 (0)3 81 81 25 31	B3
Les Marais, 4 Grande rue - 25660 SAÔNE Tel: 0033 (0)3 81 55 70 64	B2
Hôtel du Champ de Foire, rue Elisée Cusenier - 25580 ETALANS Tel: 0033 (0)3 81 59 21 01	B2
Auberge De Poudrey, Bld Puits de Poudrey - 25580 ETALANS Tel: 0033 (0)3 81 59 20 43	B2

Useful Contacts

Doctor

Jannin Decreuse Marie-Laure, 19 r Champs de Foire - 25580 ETALANS
Tel: 0033 (0)3 81 59 27 57

Farrier

Bolmont Gaetan, 3 r DE L EGLISE - 25360 GONSANS Mobile: 0033 (0)6 71 72 89 90

Hotel/B&B	Price
M. GAULARD Michel, 19, rue du Stade - 25580 VERNIERFONTAINE Tel: 0033 (0)3 81 60 01 27	B2
Le Coin du Bois - 25580 NODS Tel: 0033 (0)3 81 60 03 79 Mobile: 0033 (0)6 08 36 28 56	B2
Gaulard Michel, 19 r Stade - 25580 VERNIERFONTAINE Tel: 0033 (0)3 81 60 01 27	B2
La Ferme du Château, 2, rue du Château - 25520 AUBONNE Tel: 0033 (0)3 81 69 90 56	B2
Gite d'Etape, Mme Joseph Foglia, 2 chemin des Moulins - 25920 MOUTHIER-HAUTE-PIERRE Tel: 0033 (0)3 81 60 91 39	B2
Hôtel La Cascade, 4 rte Gorges de Noailles - 25920 MOUTHIER HAUTE PIERRE Tel: 0033 (0)3 81 60 95 30 hotellacascade@wanadoo.fr www.hotel-lacascade.fr	B3
Gérard DAUMERIE, 14 route des Gorges de Noailles - 25920 MOUTHIER HAUTE PIERRE Tel: 0033 (0)3 81 60 98 53 gerarddaumerie@aol.com	B1
Gite de Miaboulet, 8 Chause des Carres - 25920 MOUTHIER HAUTE PIERRE Tel: 0033 (0)3 81 60 98 99	B1
PR Hotel Restaurant Les Sources de la Loue, 13 Grande Rue - 25520 OUHANS Tel: 0033 (0)3 81 69 90 06	B2
Auberge Paysanne Franc-Comtoise, 18 rue du Stade - 25580 VERNIERFONTAINE Tel: 0033 (0)3 81 60 05 21 www.auberge-paysanne.fr/index.html	B2

Camping	Price
Essi les Oyes, rte de Besançcon - 25920 MOUTHIER HAUTE PIERRE Tel: 0033 (0)3 81 60 91 39	B1

Etalans to Ouhans 29.0 km

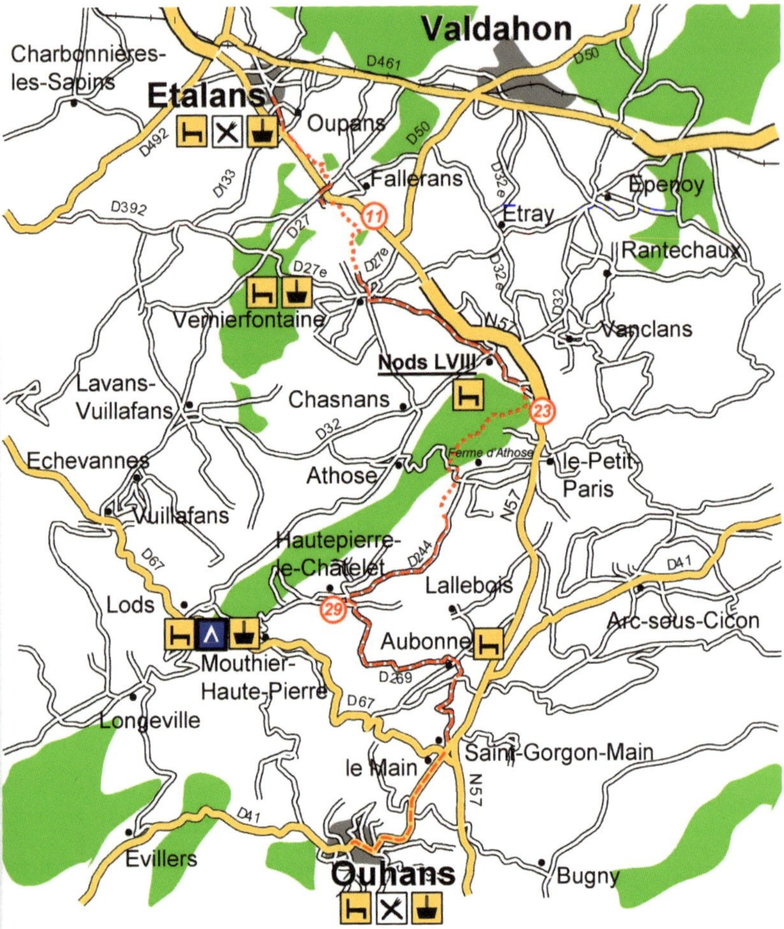

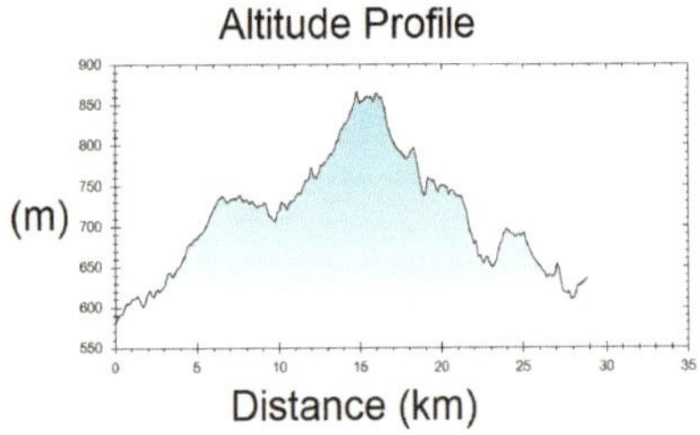

Sign to Look Out For

Route Summary: the section substantially avoids the very busy but more direct N57 by taking farm and woodland tracks and minor roads. The D41 into Ouhans, while generally quiet, may attract faster traffic.

Distance from Canterbury: 788km **Distance to Rome:** 1288km

Ascent: 607m **Descent:** 550m

Way Point N°	Way Point Distance (metres)	Total Distance (kilometres)	Directions	Verification Point	Compass	Altitude (metres)
31.01	0	0	From the crossroads Grande Rue/rue de la Gare go straight ahead direction Pontarlier	D469	SE	580
31.02	400	0.4	Continue straight ahead passing the turning off on the D133	Fontaine de la Pissoir	S	591
31.03	200	0.6	Bear right towards the main road	Garage Tournoux on left	S	601
31.04	200	0.8	At the intersection with the N57 bear left and remain on the left side	Direction Pontarlier	SE	604
31.05	600	1.4	Bear left onto a narrow unmade road		SE	613
31.06	400	1.8	At fork bear left and then bear right		SE	604
31.07	200	2.0	Bear right, continue on partially made road		SE	619
31.08	400	2.4	At crossroads turn right and proceed on the brige over the N57	VF sign	SW	623
31.09	500	2.9	Take second turn to the left on minor road	VF sign	SE	629
31.10	200	3.1	At T-junction turn left	Track across fields	SE	643
31.11	1100	4.2	Turn right through a gap in the hedge and continue straight ahead across further field		SW	676

Etalans to Ouhans 29.0 km

Way Point N°	Way Point Distance (metres)	Total Distance (kilometres)	Directions	Verification Point	Compass	Altitude (metres)
31.12	120	4.3	At corner of field continue straight into the woods through a gap in the trees	VF sign	W	678
31.13	120	4.4	Turn left immediately after woods		S	678
31.14	60	4.5	Proceed straight ahead onto track	VF sign	S	681
31.15	900	5.4	Track comes out onto minor road	Large barn on left	SE	703
31.16	400	5.8	At T-junction turn right into Vernierfontaine	Grande Rue	SW	722
31.17	120	5.9	At T-junction turn left onto the D27e	Fromagerie de Vernier on left	SE	726
31.18	50	5.0	Turn left direction Nods	Rue du Stade	E	729
31.19	300	6.3	At the crossroads straight ahead direction Nods	Rue du Stade	SE	737
31.20	3500	9.8	In Nods (LVIII) straight ahead on Grande rue	Pharmacy on left	SE	708
31.21	600	10.4	Bear right and ignore No Entry sign	VF sign	SE	722
31.22	90	10.5	Fork right between houses	VF sign	S	721
31.23	400	10.9	Bear right into trees	VF sign	SW	733
31.24	1600	12.5	Straight ahead	VF sign	SW	775
31.25	700	13.2	At junction turn left	Direction les Fermes d'Athose	SE	787
31.26	500	13.7	Turn right towards farm - Champey	VF sign	SW	820
31.27	700	14.4	Continue onto farm track	Farm on left - Sémont	SE	852
31.28	300	14.7	Track comes on to a T-junction with minor road, turn right on D244	VF sign	SW	853

Way Point N°	Way Point Distance (metres)	Total Distance (kilometres)	Directions	Verification Point	Compass	Altitude (metres)
31.29	4000	18.7	At crossroads on entry to Hautpierre-le-Châtelet, turn left	D269 direction Aubonne	SE	796
31.30	4100	22.8	In Aubonne turn left, then right down the hill	Grande Rue	SE	663
31.31	150	22.9	Remain on D269 to St-Gorgon-Main	Rue de l'Eglise to the left	S	656
31.32	1500	24.4	Bear right direction la Main, D269		S	687
31.33	600	25.0	At crossroads bear right, remain on D41	Direction Ouhans	SW	691
31.34	4000	29.0	Arrive in Ouhans			636

Ouhans to Pontarlier 18.0 km

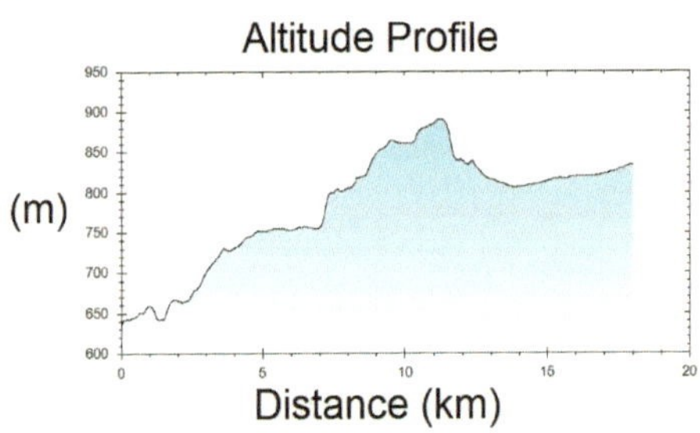

Sign to Look Out For

Route Summary: this short section is undertaken on roads, initially quiet, but becoming much busier as Pontarlier is approached.
In Pontarlier **look out for:**
The Triumphal arch of the Porte Saint-Pierre (18th century)
The Gate of the ancient church of the Annonciades (18th century)
Stained glass created in 1976 by painter Alfred Manessier for Saint-Bénigne Church.

Distance from Canterbury: 817km **Distance to Rome:** 1259km

Ascent: 339m **Descent:** 138m

Way Point N°	Way Point Distance (metres)	Total Distance (kilometres)	Directions	Verification Point	Compass	Altitude (metres)
32.01	0	0.0	At the junction between Grande Rue and rue du Château in Ouhans continue straight ahead on Grande Rue		SW	636
32.02	70	0.1	Fork left to follow D259 to Goux-les-Usiers		SW	640
32.03	4200	4.3	In Goux-les-Usiers bear right direction Bians-les-Usiers, D259	Grande Rue	SW	743
32.04	1300	5.6	Straight ahead direction Sombacour, D259	Church on left	SW	754
32.05	1400	6.0	At crossroads turn left direction Pontarlier	D6	SE	755
32.06	5700	12.7	At T-junction, turn left direction Pontarlier, D72		E	815
32.07	2500	15.2	At roundabout go straight ahead towards Pontarlier	D72	E	816
32.08	600	15.8	At roundabout continue on rue de Salins to the centre of Pontarlier		SE	819
32.09	1900	17.7	In front of town gate turn right on rue du Docteur Grenier	Porte St Pierre	S	830
32.10	80	17.8	At crossroads turn left on place Roger Solengro		SE	831
32.11	30	17.8	Bear right on rue Marpaud		SE	831
32.12	200	18.0	Arrive at the Office de Tourisme in Pontarlier (LVII)			834

Ouhans to Pontarlier 18.0 km

Hotel/B&B	Price
Ferme Hotel de la Vrine, La Vrine - 25520 GOUX LES USIERS Tel: 0033 (0)9 79 59 43 75	B2
Hôtel Saint Pierre, 3 pl St Pierre - 25300 PONTARLIER Tel: 0033 (0)3 81 46 50 80 www.hotel-st-pierre-pontarlier.com/hotel_restaurant.html	B2
Hotel du Park,1 rue Moulin Parnet - 25300 PONTARLIER Tel: 0033 (0)3 81 46 85 92	B2
Hôtel Formule, ZI Combes Sourchet r Eiffel - 25300 PONTARLIER Tel: 0033 (0)8 91 70 53 58	B2
Restaurant Hôtel Bar de Morteau, 26 r Jeanne d'Arc - 25300 PONTARLIER Tel: 0033 (0)3 81 39 14 83	B2
Hôtel de Morteau, 26 r Jeanne d'Arc - 25300 PONTARLIER Tel: 0033 (0)3 81 39 14 83 hoteldemorteau@wanadoo.fr	B2

Youth Hostel	Price
Auberge de Jeunesse, 2 r Jouffroy - 25300 PONTARLIER Tel: 0033 (0)3 81 39 06 57 pontarlier@fuaj.org	B1

Camping	Price
Camping le Larmont, r Toulombief - 25300 PONTARLIER Tel: 0033 (0)3 81 46 23 33	B1

Equestrian

Poney Club du Larmont Crins de Lune, r Toulombief - 25300 PONTARLIER
Tel: 0033 (0)3 81 46 71 67

Useful Contacts

Tourist/Information Offices

Office de Tourisme, 14 Bis r Gare - 25300 PONTARLIER Tel: 0033 (0)3 81 46 48 33

Doctor

Michaud Jean-Marie, 5 imp Canal - 25300 PONTARLIER Tel: 0033 (0)3 81 39 22 24

Farrier

Rolet Gilles, 1 r Sapins 25270 VILLERS SOUS CHALAMONT
Tel: 0033 (0)3 81 69 60 77

Veterinary

Jeannin Gérard, 7 r Doct Grenier - 25300 PONTARLIER Tel: 0033 (0)3 81 39 18 47

Hotel/B&B	Price
Le Montagnon, 20 Ter Grande Rue 25300 LES FOURGS Tel: 0033 (0)3 81 69 44 03	B2
le Fjord, Le Fjord, Grand Rue 97 1454 L'AUBERSON Tel: 0041 (0)24 454 44 26	B2
Hôtel de France, 25, rue Centrale CH-1450 SAINTE-CROIX Tel: 0041 (0)24 454 38 21 www.hotel-defrance.ch info@hotel-defrance.ch	B3

Youth Hostel	Price
Youth Hostel Ste Croix, rue Centrale 18 1450 STE-CROIX Tel: 0041 (0) 24 454 18 10 bookingoffice@youthhostel.ch www.youthhostel.ch	B1

By the Time you reach Ste Croix, you will be in SWITZERLAND. Ste Croix is a small village up in the Jura and just after the French border. Its claim to fame is its 200-year history of making musical boxes, on show at the surprisingly diverting Musée du CIMA (Centre International de la Méchanique d'Art). Northeast of Sainte-Croix, a sharp-edged ridge culminates in Mont Chasseron (1607m), one of the highest of Jura peaks.

Pontarlier to Sainte-Croix 23.3 km

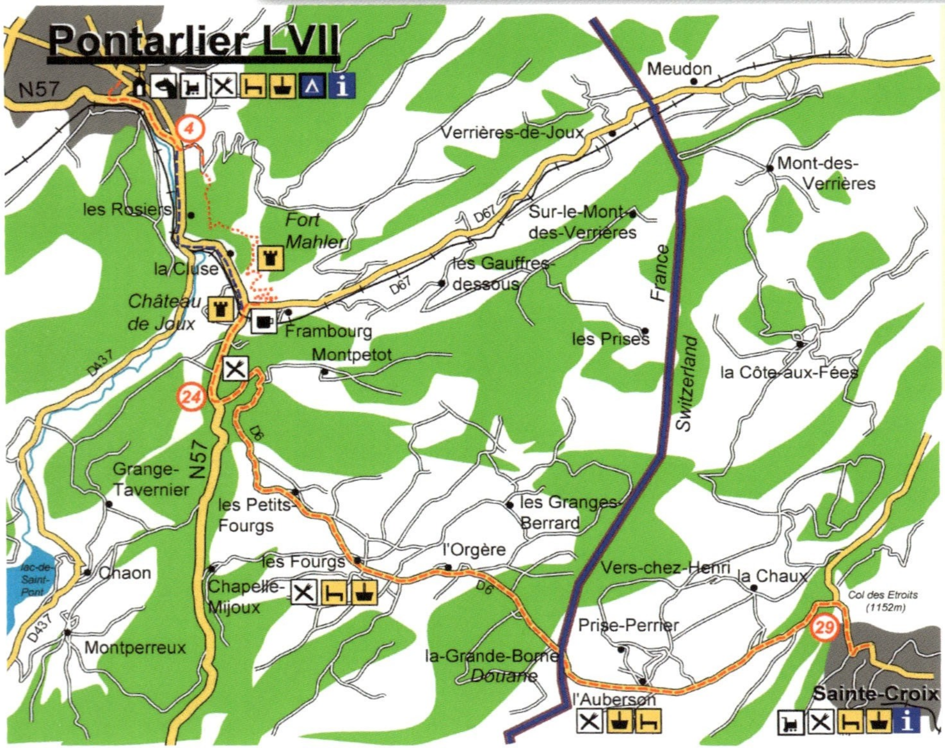

Route Summary: this is a strenuous section climbing to 1152 metres. The initial climb and descent can be avoided by remaining on the unpleasant N57 for 5.5 kilometres - cyclists may prefer this option. For those taking the off-road option the prize is a great view of Château de Joux from above. After the routes rejoin the route follows the D6 on a steady climb to the border post and eventually the Col des Etroits before commencing the descent to Sainte-Croix. A Grand Randonée route connects Frambourg to les Fourgs, but it has shown to be overgrown and extremely difficult for all groups. There are tourist facilities in each village along the D6.

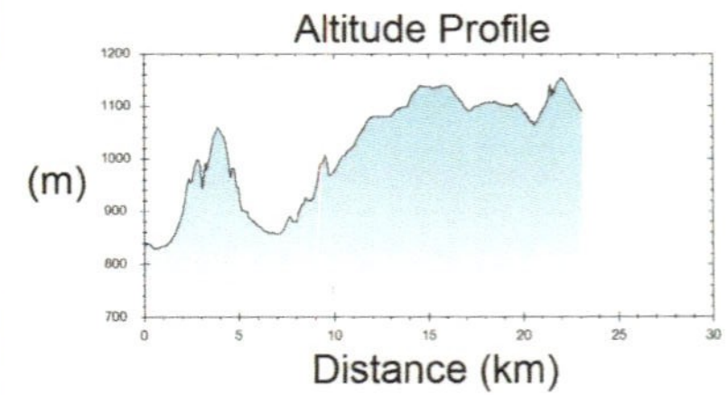

Distance from Canterbury: 835km **Distance to Rome:** 1241km

Ascent: 862m **Descent:** 608m

Way Point N°	Way Point Distance (metres)	Total Distance (kilometres)	Directions	Verification Point	Compass	Altitude (metres)
33.01	0	0.0	From the tourist office take rue de la Gare	Tourist Office on right, Post Office on left	SW	834
33.02	90	0.1	Take the last exit left from the roundabout		SE	833
33.03	1200	1.3	At roundabout go straight ahead direction Vallorbe		SE	838
33.04	80	1.4	At zebra crossing turn left. **Note:** the route ahead is passable for all but involves a strenuous off-road climb (250metres) and is particularly difficult for cyclists. However, the route provides dramatic views of the Château de Joux. For a shorter and less strenuous route remain on the busy N57 to waypoint #2	Chemin du Larmont, keep Alimentaire Discount on right	SE	841
33.05	700	2.1	Turn right onto gravel track	Direction le Fort de Mahler	S	908
33.06	60	2.1	Turn left up hill on gravel track	Enter woodland	SE	914
33.07	160	2.3	Turn right at the top of the steep climb	Blue and yellow sign	S	955
33.08	160	2.5	Continue on main track up the hill		S	954
33.09	160	2.6	Fork right to go up a slight rise		SE	974
33.10	40	2.6	Bear right remaining on the track		S	983
33.11	170	2.8	Take the right fork	First point on the route above 1000 metres	S	1000
33.12	160	3.0	Fork left onto a narrow track		S	979

Pontarlier to Sainte-Croix 23.3 km

Way Point N°	Way Point Distance (metres)	Total Distance (kilometres)	Directions	Verification Point	Compass	Altitude (metres)
33.13	30	3.0	Take right fork		S	969
33.14	50	3.1	Turn left to follow cliff edge, steep drop on right	View of Château de Joux ahead	E	945
33.15	10	3.1	Fork right following the edge of the cliff		NE	946
33.16	70	3.1	The narrow track brings you back out onto the main track, turn right up the hill		E	967
33.17	110	3.3	Bear right and continue up the hill		SE	990
33.18	300	3.5	Fork left to continue up the hill	VF Cairn, add to it!	SE	1020
33.19	60	3.6	Continue straight ahead	Summit cairn 1062 metres	E	1029
33.20	200	3.8	Turn right down the hill	Château ahead	S	1057
33.21	600	4.4	Bear left down the hill	Bar L'Estoril	S	971
33.22	500	4.9	Turn right after wire gate	N57	W	867
33.23	200	5.1	Turn left to proceed over the level crossing	Bar/hotel on the corner	S	860
33.24	1700	6.8	Turn left direction Les Fourgs, D6	Rue du Tillot and les Petits Fourgs to the left	SE	894
33.25	3500	10.3	Continue on D6	D6	SE	1052
33.26	1800	12.1	Continue through les Fourgs	la Grande-Borne	SE	1082
33.27	4500	16.6	At customs post go straight ahead		E	1102
33.28	3000	19.6	Continue through l'Auberson	Col des Etroits	NE	1100
33.29	2700	22.3	Continue straight ahead		SE	1144
33.30	1000	23.3	Arrive in Sainte-Croix centre			1095

Hotel/B&B	**Price**
Hôte1. de l'Ours Mme Chevalley Haiyan - 1445 VUITEBOEUF Tel: 0041 (0)24 459 22 59 eric.chevalley@freesurf.ch	B2
Hôtel Du Lac, 25 rue des Cygnes - 1400 YVERDON-LES-BAINS Tel: 0041 (0)24 425 23 07 info@hoteldulacyverdon.ch	B2
Gîte du Passant, rue du Parc 14 1400 - YVERDON-LES-BAINS Tel: 0041 (0)24 / 425 12 33 info@gite-du-passant.ch	B2
Hôtel du Chasseur, Place du Marché- ORBE Tel: 0041 (0)24 442 99 00 a.troyon@bluewin.ch	B2
Hôtel des Mosaïques, Mont-Choisi, Norden - 1350 ORBE Tel: 0041 (0)24 441 62 61 info@hotel-des-mosaiques.ch	B3

Religious Hostel	**Price**
Catholic Mission, 14, rue Maison-Rouge - 1400 YVERDON-LES-BAINS Tel: 0041 (0)24 424 20 50 paroisse.yverdon@cath-vd.ch www.federation.ch/paroisses/yverdon	Donation
Paroisse catholique Orbe, 1, chemin de la Dame - 1350 ORBE Tel: 0041 (0)24 441 32 90 paroisse.orbe@cath-vd.ch	Donation

Camping	**Price**
Camping des Iris, avenue des Iris - 1400 YVERDON-LES-BAINS Tel: 0041 (0)24 425 1089	B1

Equestrian

Ecurie de la Poudrière Manège d'Yverdon, 200 rue des Moulins - 1400 YVERDON-LES-BAINS Tel: 0041 (0)24 420 10 89 Mobile: 0041 (0)79 669 96 79
kohnkedavid@hotmail.com

Sainte-Croix to Orbe 37.7 km

Signs to Look Out For

Route Summary: this is a long section but offers the opportunity to either reduce the length by bypassing Yverdon-les-Bains or break the section at Yverdon. Through Switzerland Route 70 of the Swiss Mobility network connects Saint-Croix to the Col Grand-Saint-Bernard. We will follow this route where it does not impose unnecessary risks or add unnecessary distance. After the descent to Vuiteboeuf the route generally follows broad farm and forest tracks and some minor roads.

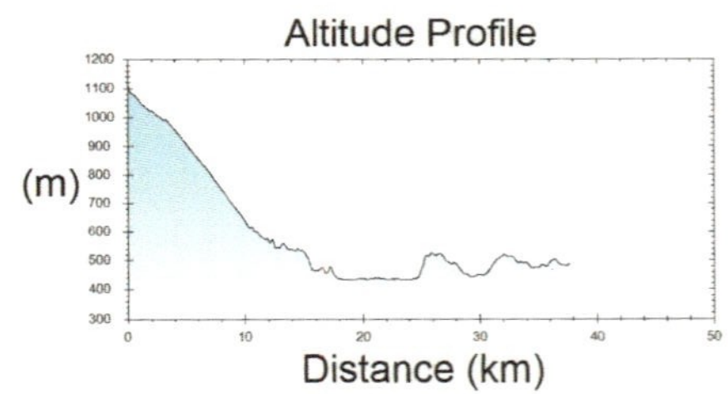

Distance from Canterbury: 859km **Distance to Rome:** 1217km

Ascent: 346m **Descent:** 973m

Way Point N°	Way Point Distance (metres)	Total Distance (kilometres)	Directions	Verification Point	Compass	Altitude (metres)
34.01	0	0.0	From place du Pont at the intersection with rue Centrale continue the descent on rue Neuve and avenue des Alpes towards Yverdon.	Tourist Office on right, Post Office on left	E	1090
34.02	3400	3.4	**Note:** on the apex of the bend beside the château de Sainte-Croix, the SwissMobility "Via Francigena" hiking Route 70 leaves the road to the right and enters the trees. The descent by this route is much steeper than the road descent and it is not recommended for cyclists or horse-riders. Hikers should give careful consideration to the conditions under foot. Route 70 crosses the road 3 times before merging with the road at the next Way Point.		SE	977
34.03	6500	9.9	Route 70 joins the road on the apex of the bend immediately above the village of Vuiteboeuf		SW	625
34.04	400	10.3	At crossroads on entry to Vuiteboeuf continue straight ahead on main road		E	597
34.05	500	10.8	At crossroads at the exit from Vuiteboeuf bear left on Route 70	Chemin de la Cantine	NE	600

Sainte-Croix to Orbe 37.7 km

Way Point N°	Way Point Distance (metres)	Total Distance (kilometres)	Directions	Verification Point	Compass	Altitude (metres)
34.06	400	11.2	Turn right between fields	Route 70	SE	596
34.07	500	11.7	Bear right to cross the road and then left on the track	Route 70	SE	574
34.08	1400	13.1	Turn left and cross the railway	Route 70	NE	540
34.09	500	13.6	Bear right to leave the trees and pass between fields	Route 70	SE	553
34.10	200	13.8	At T-junction turn left, towards Mornens	Route 70	NE	535
34.11	170	13.0	In the hamlet of Mornens turn right	Route 70	SE	540
34.12	300	14.3	Turn right and keep the trees on your left	Route 70	S	536
34.13	200	14.5	Turn left into Bois de Lily	Route 70	E	528
34.14	800	15.3	Bear right on the track	Route 70	SE	511
34.15	300	15.6	Continue straight ahead towards the railway	Route 70	SE	483
34.16	130	15.7	Take the bridge over the railway	Route 70	SE	475
34.17	120	15.8	Bear left between railway and trees	Route 70	E	465
34.18	500	16.3	Bear left and then right after crossing the railway	Route 70	E	464
34.19	300	16.6	Bear right in the centre of Valeyres-sous-Montagny	Route 70	SE	477
34.20	300	16.9	Take the right fork and cross the railway track	Route 70	S	451

Way Point N°	Way Point Distance (metres)	Total Distance (kilometres)	Directions	Verification Point	Compass	Altitude (metres)
34.21	400	17.3	At the road junction go straight ahead towards Montagny-prés-Yverdon on chemin du Temple	Route 70	S	482
34.22	200	17.5	Bear right and then left along chemin des Secrétaires	Route 70	S	462
34.23	110	17.6	Bear left and then take the right fork – chemin des Haies	Route 70	SE	451
34.24	200	17.8	Cross the main road and take the track opposite and little to the right	Route 70	S	440
34.25	600	18.4	Turn sharp left on the track and then bear right beside the main road. - If you wish to bypass Yverdon-les-Bains (saving 5.5km) keep straight ahead on the track to rejoin the main route at Way Point #36	Route 70	NE	432
34.26	600	19.0	At roundabout continue straight ahead	Pass under motorway	E	433
34.27	900	19.9	At T-junction turn right on avenue de Grandson		SE	435
34.28	600	20.5	Cross narrow canal and continue straight ahead	Rue de Neuchâtel to rue des Remparts	SE	435
34.29	900	21.4	Arrive in the centre of Yverdon. To continue to Orbe retrace route on rue des Ramparts to the previous way point.	Railway station and Tourist Information Office to the left	NW	436

Sainte-Croix to Orbe 37.7 km

Way Point N°	Way Point Distance (metres)	Total Distance (kilometres)	Directions	Verification Point	Compass	Altitude (metres)
34.30	900	22.3	At the canal crossing, cross the road turn left to continue on the cycle path beside canal.	Tourisme Pédestre sign	SW	435
34.31	400	22.7	At road junction take pedestrian crossing to remain on cycle track	Tourisme Pédestre sign	SW	435
34.32	130	22.9	At crossroads remain on the cycle path	Rue de Canal	SW	435
34.33	300	23.2	At T-junction turn right on rue de Montagny	Tourisme Pédestre sign	NW	434
34.34	500	23.7	Pass by a small industrial estate at T-junction turn left then continue straight ahead under the road bridge		SW	435
34.35	600	24.3	Turn right at T-junction	Tourisme Pédestre sign, plastic greenhouses on left	NW	433
34.36	200	24.5	Turn left direction Chamblon	Shown as a 20 minute walk on the Tourisme Pèdestre sign	S	433
34.37	60	24.5	Turn right in front a group of houses	Tourisme Pédestre sign	W	433
34.38	700	25.2	Turn left direction Chamblon	Tourisme Pèdestre sign, grass track going up the hill	S	444
34.39	400	25.6	Join road and turn left towards Chamblon	Tourisme Pédestre sign	S	515
34.40	200	25.8	Turn right with church on left	Tourisme Pédestre sign	W	521
34.41	190	26.0	Fork left onto rue des Chandelénes	Tourisme Pédestre sign	SW	524

Way Point N°	Way Point Distance (metres)	Total Distance (kilometres)	Directions	Verification Point	Compass	Altitude (metres)
34.42	180	26.2	At crossroads proceed straight ahead towards a cemetery on chemin du Pérou	Tourisme Pédestre sign	SW	516
34.43	1200	27.4	Fork right onto unmade track, direction Orbe	Tourisme Pédestre sign	W	491
34.44	900	28.3	Turn left onto a small concrete road	Turn down the hill	S	473
34.45	160	28.4	Turn sharp right down the hill	Tourisme Pédestre sign	W	464
34.46	300	28.8	At crossroads in track, proceed straight ahead onto grass track	Tourisme Pédestre sign	NW	446
34.47	600	29.4	Grass track comes onto concrete track at crossroads, turn left	Tourisme Pédestre sign	SW	439
34.48	600	29.9	At T-junction, turn right off concrete track and onto road	Tourisme Pédestre sign	NW	447
34.49	200	30.2	In Mathod, bear left direction Orbe. - Route 70 turns right at this point to make an unnecessary loop via Saint Christophe and Rances (an additional 2.8km) returning at Way Point #54	Tourisme Pédestre sign	SW	446
34.50	400	30.6	Turn right to cross small river onto rue des Champs du Pont	Tourisme Pédestre sign	W	444
34.51	1000	31.6	Continue on grass track with trees directly to your right	Tourisme Pédestre sign	SW	504

Sainte-Croix to Orbe 37.7 km

Way Point N°	Way Point Distance (metres)	Total Distance (kilometres)	Directions	Verification Point	Compass	Altitude (metres)
34.52	400	31.9	Turn right into the woods on grass track	Tourisme Pédestre sign	SW	513
34.53	400	32.3	At T-junction turn left	Yellow arrow	SW	516
34.54	300	32.6	Continue straight ahead direction Orbe	Tourisme Pédestre sign	SW	514
34.55	200	32.8	Turn right onto concrete road	Tourisme Pédestre sign	SW	513
34.56	90	32.9	Turn left onto grass track	Tourisme Pédestre sign	SE	513
34.57	300	33.2	At end of field turn right onto concrete road	Tourisme Pédestre sign	SW	495
34.58	800	34.0	Bear right and then turn sharp left onto minor road	Tourisme Pédestre sign	SE	495
34.59	170	34.2	Turn left to go under road bridge	Tourisme Pédestre sign	SE	488
34.60	400	34.6	Turn right onto track between fields	Tourisme Pédestre sign	S	469
34.61	600	35.2	Turn right with main road on the left	Tourisme Pédestre sign	NW	474
34.62	200	35.4	Turn left over road bridge. - Roman Mosaics site to the right	Tourisme Pédestre sign	SW	486
34.63	60	35.5	Cross straight over road to continue on the Sentier Pèdestre	Tourisme Pédestre sign	SW	486
34.64	300	35.8	Turn right keeping trees to the left	Tourisme Pédestre sign	W	474
34.65	140	35.9	Turn left onto rte du Signal	Tourisme Pédestre sign	S	481

Way Point N°	Way Point Distance (metres)	Total Distance (kilometres)	Directions	Verification Point	Compass	Altitude (metres)
34.66	900	36.8	Turn left with College Montchoisi directly in front	Route de Viaeyres	S	492
34.67	200	37.0	At roundabout take last exit, direction Orbe centre	Cycle path, avenue de Thienne	S	486
34.68	400	37.4	At roundabout 2nd exit, direction Chavornay	Rue des Terreaux	S	572
34.69	300	37.7	Arrive Orbe centre			571

Useful Contacts

Tourist/Information Offices

Office du tourisme d'Orbe, rue de la Poste 2 1350 ORBE Tel: 0041 (0)24 441 52 66
tourisme@orbe.ch http://tourisme.orbe.ch/accueil.php

Spa and Tourist Office, av. de la Gare 2 CH-1401 Yverdon-les-Bains
Tel: 0041 (0)24 423 61 01 info@yverdon-les-bains.ch
http://www.yverdonlesbains-tourisme.ch/e/contact/

Doctor

Chapallaz Suzanne, promenade J.J. Rousseau 8 1400 YVERDON-LES-BAINS
Tel: 0041 (0)24 426 04 62

Lasserre Murielle (-Baum), rue Sainte-Claire 3 1350 ORBE Tel: 0041 (0)24 441 22 55

Veterinary

Jutzeler Marc, avenue des Sports 5 1400 YVERDON-LES-BAINS
Tel: 0041 (0)24 426 30 30

Cabinet vétérinaire des Ducats A. Meystre et D. Hiltbrand, chemin des Ducats 1350 ORBE
Tel: 0041 (0)24 441 40 00

Farrier

Barbey Michaël, chemin des Noisetiers 17 1563 DOMPIERRE
Mobile: 0041 (0)78 614 79 15

Orbe to Lausanne 38.2 km

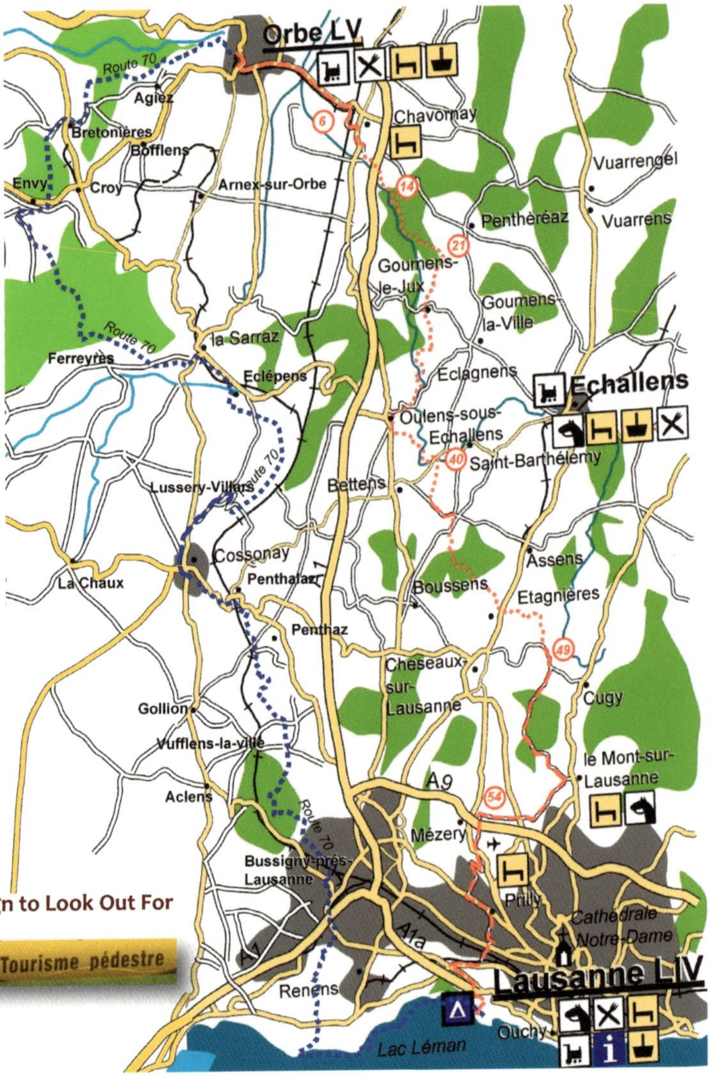

Sign to Look Out For

Tourisme pédestre

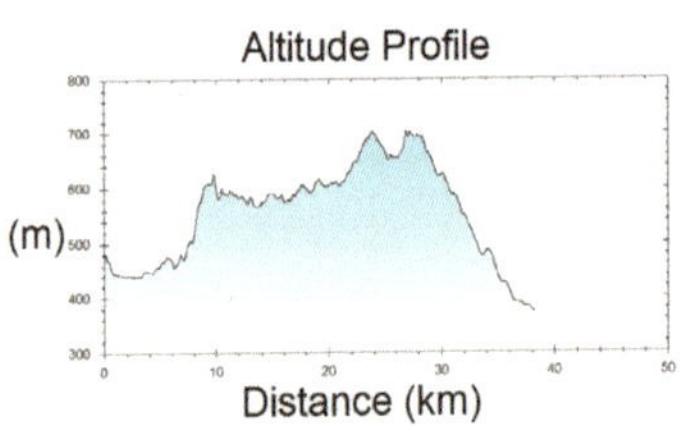

Orbe to Lausanne Pedestrian Route Altitudes

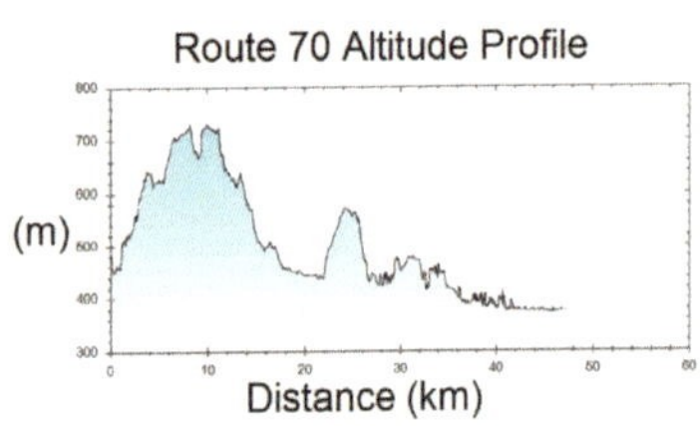

Orbe to Lausanne Route 70 Altitudes

Route Summary: this long section is substantially undertaken on farm tracks and minor roads, before entering Lausanne on generally quiet suburban streets. Route 70 adds 9 kilometres to the journey making an unacceptably long section. However Route 70 rejoins the main route on the shores of the lake at Way Point #71

Distance from Canterbury: 896km **Distance to Rome:** 1180
Ascent: 573m **Descent:** 685m

Way Point N°	Way Point Distance (metres)	Total Distance (kilometres)	Directions	Verification Point	Compass	Altitude (metres)
35.01	0	0.0	From the crossroads between rue de la Poste and rue des Terreaux take rue de la Gare towards the railway station. - for Route 70 return on rue des Terreaux and the turn left and descend towards the river on Passage du Puisoir		S	484
35.02	120	0.1	Turn left on avenue Donat-Golaz	Railway track on right	SE	475
35.03	170	0.3	At the crossroads turn right to take bridge direction Lausanne/Chavornay	Rue du Grand Pont	SW	475
35.04	170	0.5	After crossing the bridge turn left direction Chavornay	Rte de Saint-Eloi	E	475
35.05	700	1.2	Turn right direction Chavornay and join cycle track on far side of road	Pass Nestlé factory on left	SE	443
35.06	2500	3.7	Turn right to cross over the main road following the cycle path and pass in front of the hotel and railway station	Industrial buildings to the right. Main railway track to the left	S	450
35.07	600	4.3	Turn left to go under the railway bridge		E	444
35.08	80	4.3	Fork left onto larger road	Rue du Château	NE	445
35.09	90	4.4	At junction turn right	Rue du Château	E	449

Orbe to Lausanne 38.2 km

Way Point N°	Way Point Distance (metres)	Total Distance (kilometres)	Directions	Verification Point	Compass	Altitude (metres)
35.10	120	4.5	At T-junction with major road turn right	Grand Rue	S	455
35.11	400	4.0	Bear left onto rue de Collège	Cafe on left	SE	460
35.12	150	5.1	Take right fork on chemin des Vignes	Tourisme Pédestre sign	S	468
35.13	300	5.4	At fork bear right, tarmac gives way to unmade road	Tourisme Pédestre sign	SE	473
35.14	600	6.0	After passing under motorway, turn right down the hill	Tourisme Pédestre sign	W	466
35.15	110	6.1	Turn left, just in front of a large white house through the courtyard and continue with woods to the right	Tourisme Pédestre sign	S	453
35.16	1600	7.7	Fork left	Tourisme Pédestre sign	SE	501
35.17	50	7.8	Turn left up the hill	Tourisme Pédestre sign	E	508
35.18	300	8.1	Turn right at the top of the steep hill	Tourisme Pédestre sign	SE	567
35.19	400	8.5	Fork right up the hill	Tourisme Pédestre sign	SE	596
35.20	300	8.8	Cross concrete road and continue on track	Proceed towards the tower	SE	606
35.21	300	9.1	Turn right at crossroads in track	Tourisme Pédestre sign	W	604
35.22	200	9.3	Turn left direction Etagnières	Tourisme Pédestre sign	S	623
35.23	170	9.4	Track emerges onto a concrete road, turn right down the hill	Tourisme Pédestre sign	S	614
35.24	190	9.6	Turn left down the hill beside golf club	Tourisme Pédestre sign	S	590
35.25	800	10.4	At T-junction turn right down the hill	Sign for Golf club Domaine de Brésil on post	SW	588

Way Point N°	Way Point Distance (metres)	Total Distance (kilometres)	Directions	Verification Point	Compass	Altitude (metres)
35.26	130	10.6	Turn left just after passing a house - Goumens-le-Jux	Tourisme Pédestre sign	SE	585
35.27	400	10.0	Bear right at fork	Tourisme Pédestre sign	S	591
35.28	600	11.6	Turn right direction Etagniérs	Tourisme Pédestre sign - track alternates between grass and concrete	SW	582
35.29	600	12.2	Turn left onto chemin du Talent, slightly up the hill and towards church spire	Tourisme Pédestre sign	SE	567
35.30	200	12.4	Bear right at fork onto concrete road	Tourisme Pédestre sign	S	578
35.31	150	12.5	Bear right between trees	Tourisme Pédestre sign	W	586
35.32	300	12.8	Track emerges onto concrete road, turn left	Pass sewage plant on right	S	565
35.33	1100	13.9	Turn right on le Riaz	Direction village Oulens-sous-Echallens	W	576
35.34	400	14.3	Bear left into village		S	589
35.35	300	14.6	Bear left on rue du Centre		S	589
35.36	160	14.8	Turn left on gravel track	Towards woods	E	588
35.37	600	15.4	Turn right in front of woods	Keep trees on left	SE	586
35.38	200	15.6	Bear left with river on left	Tourisme Pédestre sign	SE	578
35.39	200	15,8	Turn right keeping farm buildings on left	Tourisme Pédestre sign	E	575
35.40	1200	16.0	At junction with more major road turn right and immediately bear left	Tourisme Pédestre sign	S	588
35.41	1200	18.2	At T-junction turn left direction Bioley-Orjulaz/Assens	Large factory at the bottom of the hill on left	SE	597

Orbe to Lausanne 38.2 km

Way Point N°	Way Point Distance (metres)	Total Distance (kilometres)	Directions	Verification Point	Compass	Altitude (metres)
35.42	500	18.7	Proceed straight ahead direction Assens		E	594
35.43	200	18.9	At crossroads turn right onto cycle track #22, just before reaching the village, then proceed direction Lausanne	Chemin de l'Entoz	S	609
35.44	300	19.2	Straight ahead following cycle route	Direction woods	S	616
35.45	600	19.8	Fork left and then bear right on chemin de la Forêt	Avoid gravel track to the left	SE	603
35.46	2400	22.2	Turn right into the village of Etagnières		S	614
35.47	300	22.5	Straight ahead towards village centre	Cycle route #22, direction Lausanne	SE	626
35.48	200	22.7	At T-junction with main road turn right and immediately left and continue to follow cycle route #22 to the outskirts of Lausanne.	Cycle route #22, direction Lausanne	SE	629
35.49	1700	24.4	Pass through Morrens and bear right on chemin de la Mèbre		S	699
35.50	3600	27.0	On entering le-Mont-sur-Lausanne turn right on route du Grand Mont		SW	695
35.51	700	28.7	Bear right on chemin de Pernessy		SW	663
35.52	700	29.4	At crossroads straight ahead	Chemin du Marais	W	627
35.53	200	29.6	Turn left onto a small concrete road in the direction of the main road. Cross the main road with care.		W	618

Way Point N°	Way Point Distance (metres)	Total Distance (kilometres)	Directions	Verification Point	Compass	Altitude (metres)
35.54	1300	30.9	At crossroads of minor roads turn left to cross motorway bridge	Chemin du Sous Bois	S	587
35.55	800	31.7	Cross over main road and then cross the railway using the pedestrian crossing		W	557
35.56	30	31.7	After crossing railway, turn left and then right down the hill		S	554
35.57	60	31.8	At crossroads turn left	Chemin du Dérochet	SE	550
35.58	400	32.1	Just before reaching railway and main road, turn right	Turn towards lake	W	538
35.59	600	32.8	Turn sharp left onto chemin de Champvent		S	519
35.60	1100	33.8	Turn left onto rte de Cossonay	Lake on the right	SE	476
35.61	700	34.5	At roundabout turn right towards the lake. - for Lausanne (LIV) centre continue straight ahead on rte de Cossonay	rte des Fumeaux	S	482
35.62	300	34.8	At fork in road bear left and immediately right on chemin de Bel Orne		S	473
35.63	500	35.3	At junction with the major rte de Renens straight ahead on avenue du Chablais	Towards lake and roundabout	SW	436
35.64	110	35.5	Straight ahead at roundabout on avenue du Chablais	Lake ahead	S	430
35.65	400	35.9	Straight ahead at roundabout on avenue du Chablais		W	425
35.66	700	36.6	Turn sharp left on rte de Chavannes	Lake on right	SE	392

Way Point N°	Way Point Distance (metres)	Total Distance (kilometres)	Directions	Verification Point	Compass	Altitude (metres)
35.67	700	37.3	At crossroads turn right on chemin du Bois Vaux and pass under main road	Towards lake	SW	389
35.68	200	37.5	At roundabout with IOC offices to the right turn left	2nd exit from roundabout leads to camp-site	SE	384
35.69	400	37.9	At the end of the road turn right between tennis courts and running track		W	379
35.70	100	38.0	Turn left onto path towards lake-shore		SW	378
35.71	190	38.2	Arrive at the shore of Lac Leman			374

Useful Contacts

Tourist/Information Offices

Lausanne Tourisme and Convention bureau, 2, avenue de Rhodanie - 1000 LAUSANNE
Tel: 0041 (0)21 613 73 73 information@lausanne-tourisme.ch
www.lausanne-tourisme.ch

Internet Cafe

Cyber-Land Suisse, Grand Pont 10 - 1007 LAUSANNE japmedia@freesurf.ch
www.cyber-land.ch

Ecole-Club, 3, rue Neuve - 1003 LAUSANNE info@ecmvd.ch

FragBox, 3, rue de la Tour- 1004 LAUSANNE

Quanta Virtual Fun Space, 4, Place de la Gare - LAUSANNE

Arobas City, 3, Tivoli - 1000 LAUSANNE

ESF - Espace Saint-Fran, 12 Place St-François 1003 LAUSANNE

Doctor

Mange Bernard, 19, avenue Alexandre-Vinet - 1004 LAUSANNE
Tel: 0041 (0)21 641 08 08

Vogel Nicolas, 40, avenue de Floréal - 1008 PRILLY Tel: 0041 (0)21 625 19 51

Veterinary

Cabinet Vétérinaire de la Charbonnière, 15, route du Chasseur - 1008 PRILLY
Tel: 0041 (0) 21 671 11 55
Cabinet vétérinaire des Bergières Vingerhoets Marc, 50, avenue Bergières - 1004 LAUSANNE Tel: 0041 (0)21 683 33 33

Farrier

Maret Cyril, 14, route de la Rippe - 231263 CRASSIER Mobile: 0041 (0)79 771 63 32

B&B/Hotel	Price
Yves, Benoit, Grand Rue - 69 1373 CHAVORNY Tel: 0041 (0)2 44 41 09 43	B2
Hôtel Central, 4, Place de Coppoz - 1052 LE MONT-SUR-LAUSANNE Tel: 0041 (0)21 652 01 46 lecentral@bluewin.ch	B2
Hotel La Croisée, 15, av. Marc Dufour - 1007 LAUSANNE Tel: 0041 (0)21 321 09 09 la.croisee@chrischona.ch	B2
Guesthouse & Backpacker, 4 chemin des Epinettes - 1007 LAUSANNE Tel: 0041 (0)21 601 80 00 info@lausanne-guesthouse.ch	B1
Bed and Breakfast, 10 Flumeaux - 1008 PRILLY Tel: 0041(0) 79 689 45 41 deillon@2wire.ch	B2
Hôtel Auberge du Cheval-Blanc Santiago Chantal, 11, route de Lausanne - 1040 ECHALLENS Tel: 0041 (0)21 881 12 96	B2
Le Break Billard, place de l'Hôtel de Ville - 1040 ECHALLENS Tel: 0041 (0)21 882 28 82	B2

Religious Hostel	Price
Paroisse Protestante, rue Blécherette - 1052 LE MONT-SUR-LAUSANNE Tel: 0041 (0)21 652 21 47	Donation

Youth Hostel	Price
Auberge de Jeunesse, 36 Ch. du Bois-de-Vaux - 1000 LAUSANNE Tel: 0041 (0)21 626 02 22 www.tiscover.ch/jeunotel	B1

Camping	Price
Camping de Vidy-Lausanne, 3, chemin du Camping - 1007 LAUSANNE Tel: 0041 (0)21 622 50 00	B1
La Carillère, 73, route du Jorat - 1000 LAUSANNE Tel: 0041 (0)21 784 46 19	B1
Pra-Collet Rod Michel, 71A, route du Jorat - 1000 LAUSANNE 26 Mobile: 0041 (0)78 623 51 pracollet@freesurf.ch	B1

Equestrian
Manège du Mont, 30, Ch. des Buchilles - 1052 LE MONT-SUR-LAUSANNE Tel: 0041 (0)21 652 99 11 manege_a_berger@bluewin.ch http://manege-du-mont.ch
Manège du Chalet à Gobet, 304, rte de Berne - 1000 LAUSANNE Tel: 0041 (0)21 784 14 34 ljohner@worldcom.ch
Ecurie des Planches, 3 chemin des Planches - 1040 ECHALLENS Tel: 0041 (0)21 881 62 68

Lausanne to Villeneuve 36.0 km

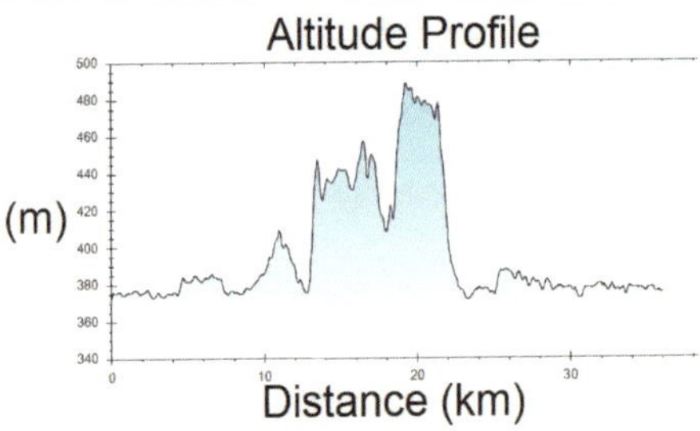

Route Summary: The route follows Route 70 by the lake shore before climbing into the vineyard terraces and then returning to the lake side in Vevey. Cyclists may wish to avoid the climb and remain on the lake-side road. At Way Point #8

Distance from Canterbury: 935km **Distance to Rome:** 1141km

Ascent: 373m **Descent:** 370m

Way Point N°	Way Point Distance (metres)	Total Distance (kilometres)	Directions	Verification Point	Compass	Altitude (metres)
36.01	0	0.0	From the lake-side take the path and cycleway to the east keeping the lake on your right	Towards the steamer quay	E	377
36.02	1500	1.5	At intersection between lake-side track and main road, avenue de Rhodanie, turn right	Continue on cycle path	SE	377
36.03	400	1.9	Turn right at roundabout with a diving figure and remain close to the lake-shore	Cycle path towards lake, Quai des Chalands	E	375
36.04	2500	4.4	Remain on road, direction Vevey	Cycle track	NE	378
36.05	150	4.5	At T-junction turn right towards Vevey		E	383
36.06	3000	7.5	Bear right through car park towards boat dock and follow lake-side		SE	376
36.07	1600	9.2	Turn left and then right to join main road	Route de Lavaux	SE	377
36.08	1500	10.7	Beside the Villettes railway station, cross the road, pass under the railway and bear right	Proceed parallel to the railway and into the vineyards	SE	388

Lausanne to Villeneuve 36.0 km

Way Point N°	Way Point Distance (metres)	Total Distance (kilometres)	Directions	Verification Point	Compass	Altitude (metres)
36.09	2300	12.9	On reaching the Cully railway station, turn right on rue de la Gare and pass under the railway	Towards the lake	SE	391
36.10	200	13.2	At the roundabout turn left on route de Vevey		E	379
36.11	600	13.8	Bear right on route de Moratel	Railway immediately to the left	E	376
36.12	130	13.9	Turn left to pass under the railway and the main road	Climb the hill with the marina behind	N	379
36.13	150	14.0	Bear right on chemin de Plan-Pérey	Continuing to climb the hill	E	399
36.14	400	14.4	On the outskirts of the village of Epesses turn right on the track, chemin del'Ouchette	Proceed parallel to the lake-shore joining chemin du Calamin	SE	454
36.15	3500	17.9	On the outskirts of the village of Rivaz turn right on Sur la Croix and immediately left on rue du Collége		E	383
36.16	200	18.1	Turn left on route des Bons Voisins and immediately right on chemin des Paleyres	Continue in the vineyards parallel to the lakeshore	E	448
36.17	1800	19.9	In Saint-Saphorin bear left up the hill on Sentier des Rondes		E	413
36.18	180	20.1	At the crossroads continue straight ahead up the hill on Sentier des Rondes		NE	441
36.19	130	20.2	At the T-junction with the road turn right and then bear left		E	463
36.20	200	20.4	At the fork bear left on chemin du Burignon	Towards railway	E	470

Way Point N°	Way Point Distance (metres)	Total Distance (kilometres)	Directions	Verification Point	Compass	Altitude (metres)
36.21	200	20.6	On the bend bear right	Parallel to the railway	E	489
36.22	300	20.9	Continue straight ahead		E	489
36.23	400	21.3	At the fork bear right on chemin des Combes		E	485
36.24	1100	22.4	Turn sharp left on chemin du Grand Pin		NE	466
36.25	180	22.6	Turn sharp right and go down hill on chemin des Rochettes	Towards Corseaux	SE	479
36.26	180	22.8	Turn left on rue du Village		SE	452
36.27	300	23.1	Turn right on chemin de la Crausaz	Parallel to the finicular	S	430
36.28	150	23.3	Turn left on chemin du Marguery		SE	407
36.29	150	23.4	Turn left on rue des Cerisiers and then bear right under the railway bridges		S	391
36.30	190	23.6	At the roundabout continue straight ahead on avenue Nestlé		S	385
36.31	130	23.7	Turn right on avenue de Savoie	Beside Nestlé offices	SW	384
36.32	170	23.9	Turn left and proceed along the lake-shore		SE	376
36.33	2200	26.1	In la Tour-de-Peilz, shortly after the lake-side road turns inland on rue du Château turn right on rue du Bourg-Dessous	Cycle Route #1	SE	381
36.34	160	26.3	Turn left onto cycle route back to the main road. Turn right at the main road junction		SE	384

Lausanne to Villeneuve 36.0 km

Way Point N°	Way Point Distance (metres)	Total Distance (kilometres)	Directions	Verification Point	Compass	Altitude (metres)
36.35	3100	29.4	At traffic lights turn right on rue du Torrent to return to lake-side and turn left	Quai de Clarens	SE	382
36.36	1900	31.3	Beside the Tourist Office in Montreux continue straight ahead on Quai de la Rouvenaz		S	372
36.37	4100	35.4	On entry to Villeneuve, bear right to remain close to the water	Leaving Cycle Route #1	SW	385
36.38	600	36.0	Arrive in Villeneuve centre beside steamer jetty			376

Useful Contacts

Tourist/Information Offices

Montreux-Vevey Tourisme, 5, rue du Théâtre - 1820 MONTREUX
Tel: 0041 (0) 848 86 84 84 www.montreuxtourism.ch

Internet Cafe

Cyberworld, 90, Grand Rue - 1820 MONTREUX Tel: 0041 (0)21 963 51 52

DIGITAL PLANET, 49, avenue du Casino - 1820 MONTREUX Tel: 0041 (0)21 961 36 71

Cyberworld, 4-6, rue du Torrent - 1800 VEVEY info@cyberworldcafe.ch

Doctor

Darmal Adam, 71, Grand Rue - 1820 MONTREUX Tel: 0041 (0)21 961 19 18

Chautems Philippe, 79, rue des Fortifications - 1844 VILLENEUVE VD
Tel: 0041 (0)21 960 24 92

Veterinary

Dardenne Philippe, 41, Grand Rue - 1844 VILLENEUVE VD Tel: 0041 (0)21 968 32 10

Schmid Natacha, 14, rue de l'Eglise Catholique - 1820 MONTREUX
Tel: 0041 (0)21 963 80 80 Mobile: 0041 (0)79 758 58 17

B&B/Hotel	Price
Hôtel de l'Ecusson Vaudois, rte de Village - 1847 RENNAZ Tel: 0041 (0)21 960 10 85	B2
Motel Restoroute de Rennaz, Junction Autoroute - 1847 RENNAZ Tel: 0041 (0)21 96040 41	B2
Hôtel du Nord Bezençon, 2, rue Colomb - 1860 AIGLE Tel: 0041 (0)24 468 10 55 info@hoteldunord.chInternet www.hoteldunord.ch	B3
Hôtel des Messageries, 19, rue du Midi - 1860 AIGLE Tel: 0041 (0)24 466 20 60	B2
Barbaro - Motel, Les Essertons - 1860 AIGLE Tel: 0041 (0)24 466 56 77	B2
Maria Ausserladschieder, 18, chemin des Charmettes - 1860 AIGLE Tel: 0041 (0)24 467 95 80	B2
Hôtel de la Gare, 66, av. de la Gare - 1870 MONTHEY Tel: 0041 (0)24 471 93 93	B2
Hôtel la Dent-du-Midi, 1, avenue Simplon - 1890 SAINT MAURICE Tel: 0041 (0)24 485 12 09	B2
Hôtel de la Gare Evionna, route Cantonale - 1902 EVIONNAZ Tel: 0041 (0)27 767 19 57	B2
Hotel de Ville, 8, rue Centrale - 1880 BEX Tel: 0041(0)24 463 2082	B2
Myriam & André Berney Jaquerod, 6, chemin de Vuarrens - 1880 BEX Tel: 0041(0) 24 466 95 25	B2
Rosemarie & Fritz Siegenthaler, 22, ave de la Gare - 1880 BEX Tel: 0041 (0)24 463 27 81	B2
Hôtel Pont du Trient, La Verrerie - 1904 VERNAYAZ Tel: 0041 (0)27 764 14 12 Mobile: 0041 (0)79 221 06 46	B2
Hôtel du Forum, 74, avenue du Grand Saint-Bernard - 1920 MARTIGNY Tel: 0041 (0)27 722 18 41 info@le-gourmet.ch	B2

Religious Hostel	Price
Abbaye de Saint-Maurice, 15, av. d'Agaune - 1890 SAINT-MAURICE Tel: 0041 (0)24 486 04 04 **Note:** groups of pilgrims only accepted on previous written agreement	B1
Les Conseils de paroisse, 3A, rue d'Oche - 1920 MARTIGNY Tel: 0041 (0)27 722 32 20 paroissep@bluewin.ch or info@paroissep.ch	Donation

Villeneuve to Martigny 40.2 km

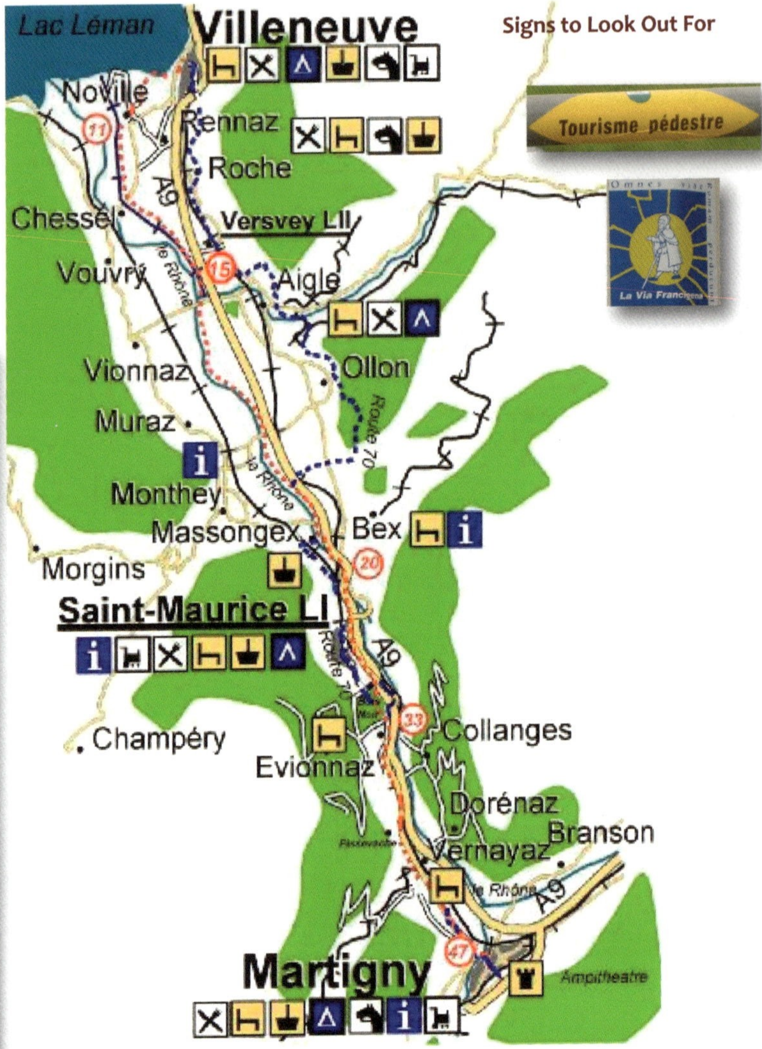

Signs to Look Out For

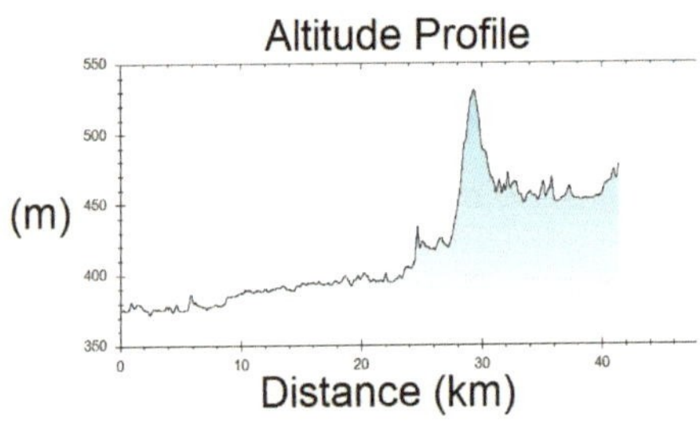

Route Summary: this very long section generally follows pleasant pathways on the side of the canal and then on the banks of the Rhone. Saint Maurice offers the opportunity for an intermediate stop, after which there is a short rugged section through the Bois Noir before returning to level tracks and minor roads passing beside the apricot orchards on the entry to Martigny. Route 70 passes directly through Aigle but hugs the base of the hills first on the east and then the western side of the valley adding distance and unnecessary climbing In Martigny **look out for:** Roman archaeological remains. The city is known for its amphitheatre, restored in 1978. Cow fights are held in the amphitheatre during early autumn for the "Comptoir". The city is also famous for its museum, the Pierre Gianadda Foundation, built on top of Roman ruins. The foundation hosts three painting exhibitions every year, with works by renowned masters. It also has permanent automobile and Gallo-Roman exhibitions.

Distance from Canterbury: 971km **Distance to Rome:** 1105km

Ascent: 385m **Descent:** 281m

Villeneuve to Martigny 40.2 km

Way Point N°	Way Point Distance (metres)	Total Distance (kilometres)	Directions	Verification Point	Compass	Altitude (metres)
37.01	0	0.0	From the steamer jetty in Villeneuve take rue du Quai with the lake to the right. **Note:** for Route 70 go straight ahead into place de la Gare, cross the railway and bear right on route d'Arvel. Route 70 will rejoin our route on the banks of the Rhone 2km before Way Point #17	Direction Noville.	SW	375
37.02	500	0.5	Turn right off the main road immediately after crossing the bridge	Towards the lake	NW	375
37.03	100	0.6	Turn left to follow the Tourisme Pèdestre sign	Keeping lake to the right	W	375
37.04	1300	1.9	Proceed straight ahead	Equestrian centre on the right	SW	372
37.05	900	2.8	At T-junction turn left	Chemin du Battoir	S	375
37.06	200	3.0	At junction in Noville turn right	Rue des Anciennes Postes	S	376
37.07	70	3.1	Take right fork	Rue des Anciennes Postes	S	376
37.08	50	3.1	Turn right on chemin des Bousses	House, la Belette, on left	S	374

Villeneuve to Martigny 40.2 km

Way Point N°	Way Point Distance (metres)	Total Distance (kilometres)	Directions	Verification Point	Compass	Altitude (metres)
37.09	80	3.2	At T-junction turn right remaining on chemin des Bousses	Tourisme Pédestre sign	SW	376
37.10	120	3.3	At junction in track turn left	Tourisme Pédestre sign	SW	375
37.11	400	3.7	Join the canal-side path and turn left		S	375
37.12	1700	5.4	As tarmac runs out and emerges onto unmade track go straight ahead remaining beside the canal	Canal on right	S	376
37.13	1200	6.6	On meeting main road, cross over to continue on the track beside the Grand Canal		SE	378
37.14	1300	7.9	Bear right over canal bridge and turn left to continue on the canal-path on the other side	Canal on left	SE	379
37.15	1300	9.2	Shortly before the next bridge turn right towards the river, then turning left to follow the riverside path. **Note:** Those wishing to visit the named village of Versvey (LII) should take the bridge and continue straight ahead for 1200 metres. The village is to the left. Rejoin the route by retracing your steps to this point		SE	383
37.16	1900	11.1	Straight ahead over the bridge	Tourisme Pedèstre signs to Aigle Centre and Aigle Gare to the left	SE	388
37.17	9900	21.0	Continue straight ahead alongside the Rhône	Equestrian Centre on left	S	395
37.18	400	21.4	Turn left onto road beside pedestrian river bridge. **Note:** Route 70 will cross the footbridge and pass through Masongex before turning left to follow the railway towards Saint-Mauricethen turn left	Holiday Camp on left	NE	395

Way Point N°	Way Point Distance (metres)	Total Distance (kilometres)	Directions	Verification Point	Compass	Altitude (metres)
37.19	80	21.5	Turn right following Pedèstre sign for St Maurice	Pass through trees and rejoin river-side path	S	400
37.20	2400	23.9	At junction with main road, cross over the road and turn right down the ramp		SE	451
37.21	130	24.0	Turn right under the road bridge and across the river bridge	The château of Saint Maurice is straight ahead	SW	482
37.22	120	24.1	Turn left in front of the château		S	447
37.23	300	24.4	On entering St Maurice (LI) fork right on avenue d'Agaune and proceed through the town. **Note:** Route 70 takes the left fork before turning right towards the station and left in the station forecourt. The route then crosses the railway bridge and proceeds on the far side of the tracks before rejoining our route Way Point #30		S	436
37.24	1500	25.9	Turn right to pass under railway bridge and proceed beside the railway	Cycle Route #1, keep railway to left after bridge	SE	425
37.25	1000	26.9	Fork right direction Bois Noir		SE	429
37.26	500	27.4	At crossroads, proceed straight ahead on chemin du Bois Noir		SE	454
37.27	300	27.8	Proceed straight ahead into woods on unmade road. **Note:** The path through the woods includes a narrow bridge which is impassable for horses. Horse riders should turn left here and pass under the motorway on the Alternate Route rejoining the main route at Waypoint #33		S	481
37.28	400	28.1	Fork right		W	511
37.29	20	28.2	Fork left		SW	512

Villeneuve to Martigny 40.2 km

Way Point N°	Way Point Distance (metres)	Total Distance (kilometres)	Directions	Verification Point	Compass	Altitude (metres)
37.30	190	28.4	At T-junction turn left		SE	522
37.31	80	28.4	Straight ahead on narrow footbridge over gorge		SE	525
37.32	600	29.0	At T-junction with road, turn left direction Evionnaz		E	515
37.33	300	29.3	Turn right to proceed parallel to the motorway. **Note:** Alternate Route rejoins from the left	Pedèstre sign	S	487
37.34	500	29.8	At crossroads go straight over and down the hill		S	473
37.35	170	30.0	Bear right and continue down the main street of Evionnaz with church on right	VF sign	S	469
37.36	300	30.3	At T-junction turn left	Cycle Route #1	S	462
37.37	60	30.4	Turn right onto a small road	VF and Martigny signs	S	460
37.38	2100	32.5	Turn right at T-junction on the edge of La Balmaz, staying close to the mountain-side on your right	VF and Martigny signs	SE	453
37.39	300	32.8	Turn right onto the main road	Cycle track	S	460
37.40	1100	33.9	Turn right towards Pisse Vache waterfalls and cross railway tracks, keep the gulley as close as possible to your right. **Note:** Riders and cyclists may prefer to avoid the path which though passable has some narrow sections - remain on the road and rejoin at Waypoint #44	VF sign.	S	451
37.41	400	34.3	Bear left to cross railway track. The track winds to go back over the railway a second time	VF sign	S	472
37.42	500	34.8	Turn left towards the road	VF sign	E	464

Way Point N°	Way Point Distance (metres)	Total Distance (kilometres)	Directions	Verification Point	Compass	Altitude (metres)
37.43	70	34.8	At crossroads turn right onto tarmac track after crossing a bridge	VF sign	SE	452
37.44	900	35.7	At junction with main road turn right towards Martigny		SE	455
37.45	700	36.4	Bear right onto farm track running parallel to road. **Note:** Route 70 progresses between the orchards and the foot of the cliffs		SE	453
37.46	2400	38.8	Track bears right towards the mountain-side		SW	458
37.47	120	38.0	Track joins road go straight ahead towards Martigny. Cross river bridge and follow rue Marc Morand	Rue de la Bâtiaz	SE	463
37.48	1200	40.2	Arrive Martigny centre			477
The Alternate Route follows the road to bypass the Bois Noir where there is a bridge which is impassable by horses						
1	0	0.0	Proceed towards the motorway and pass under road bridge	Direction Noville.	NE	480
2	300	0.3	At T-junction turn right	Towards the lake	SE	457
3	500	0.8	Bear right down ramp to proceed back under motorway towards woods	Keeping lake to the right	SW	464
4	180	1.0	After passing under motorway turn left	Equestrian centre on the right	S	477
5	700	1.7	Rejoin route at Way Point #33 proceeding straight ahead towards Evionnaz	Chemin du Battoir		485

Camping	Price
Camping des Farettes, chemin de l'Ecluse 39 1860 AIGLE Tel: 0041 (0)24 466 19 68	B1
Les Neuvilles, rue du Levant 68 1920 MARTIGNY Tel: 0041 (0)27 722 45 44	B1

Equestrian

Manège et école d'équitation, 1. de Rennaz Mingard Catherine 1847 RENNAZ
Tel: 0041 (0)21 960 22 65   Mobile 0041 (0)79 412 20 67

Manège des Ilôts 1920 MARTIGNY   Tel: 0041 (0)27 722 85 07
Mobile: 0041 (0)79 628 70 51   ecuriedarioly@bluewin.ch

Villeneuve to Martigny 40.2 km

Useful Contacts

Tourist/Information Offices

Office de Tourisme, Pl. Centrale 3 1870 MONTHEY Tel: 0041 (0)24 475 79 63
monthey.tourisme@bluemail.ch www.chablais.info

Saint-Maurice Tourisme, 1, avenue des Terreaux 1890 SAINT-MAURICE
Tel: 0041 (0)24 485 40 40 tourisme@st-maurice.ch   www.saint-maurice.ch

Office du tourisme de Bex, rue de la Gare 24 1880 BEX info@bex-tourisme.ch
www.bex-tourisme.ch

Office du tourisme, avenue de la Gare 6 1920 MARTIGNY Tel: 0041 (0)27 720 49 49
info@martignytourism.ch www.martigny.com

Internet Cafe

Casino Cyber Café, av. de la Gare 17 1920 MARTIGNY

Doctor

Cornut Josy-Philippe, rue Principale 1902 EVIONNAZ Tel: 0041 (0)27 767 14 00

Moillen Marcel, avenue de la Gare 10 1920 MARTIGNY Tel: 0041 (0)27 723 25 50

Veterinary

Cabinet vétérinaire de l'Europe Dewarrat André, avenue de l'Europe 64 1870 MONTHEY Tel: 0041 (0)24 472 42 32

Daves Christine, chemin du Milieu 50 1920 MARTIGNY Tel: 0041 (0)27 722 08 66

B&B/Hotel	Price
Hôtel de la Gare - 1933 SEMBRANCHER Tel: 0041 (0)27 785 11 14 hotelgaresembrancher@bluewin.ch	B2
Hôtel de l'Union, Place Centrale - 1937 ORSIERES Tel: 0041 (0)27 783 11 38 info@chezjo.ch	B2
Hôtel Terminus, Place de la Gare - 1937 ORSIERES Tel: 0041 (0)27 783 20 40 terminus@dransnet.ch	B2
B&B Marie-Claude Tornay, rte de Senaire - 1937 ORSIERES Tel: 0041 (0)27 783 10 12	B2

Camping	Price
Camping La Prairie, rte du Grand-St-Bernard - 1933 SEMBRANCHER Tel: 0041 (0) 27 785 21 30	B1

Religious Hostel	Price
Paroisse Orsières, Place de l'Eglise - 1937 ORSIÈRES Tel: 0041 (0)27 783 11 44 paroisse@orsieres.com	Donation

Useful Contacts

Tourist/Information Offices

Au Pays du Saint-Bernard, 92, rte de la Gare - 1937 ORSIÈRES
Tel: 0041 (0)27 783 32 48 info@saint-bernard.ch www.saint-bernard.ch

Transport on the Great St Bernard Pass

St Bernard Express (Train and bus), 3, rue de la Poste - 1920 MARTIGNY
Tel: 0041 (0)27 721 68 40 pascal.may@tmrsa.chwww.sbb.ch

Great St Bernard Taxis Tel: 0041 (0)79 217 08 27 or 0041 (0)76 222 43 43
mathieu.j.c@gmail.com

Weather Forecast Great St Bernard Pass

METEORISK Tel: 0041(0)27 323 64 02 http://www.meteo-valais.ch/

Martigny to Orsières 20.2 km

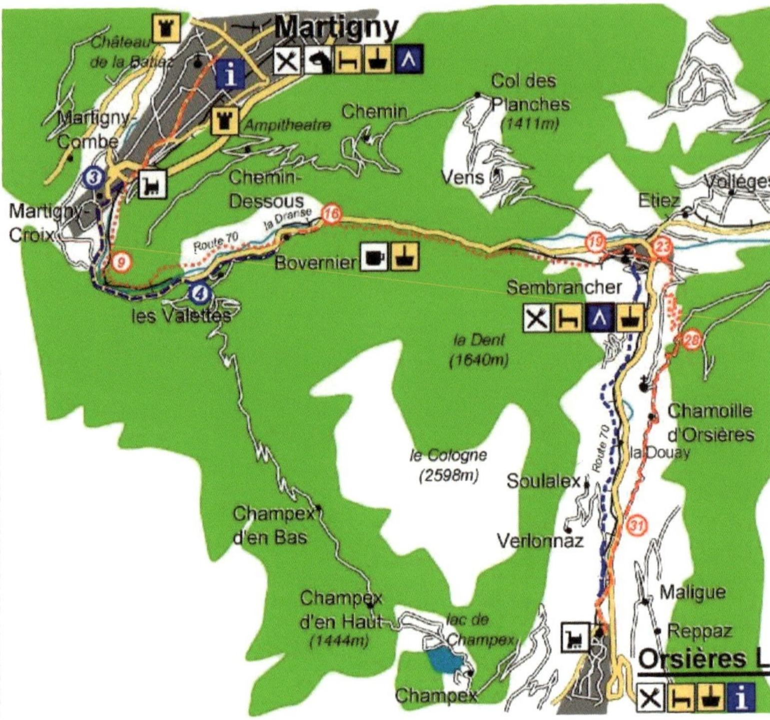

Signs to Look Out For

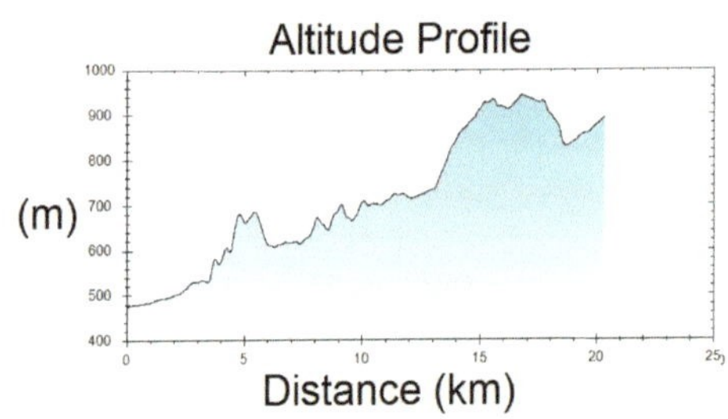

Route Summary: after leaving Martigny the route takes to a narrow track with steep ascents. This section is forbidden to horse-riders and cyclists. Forest tracks connect Bovernier and Sembrancher. After Sembrancher there is the choice of Route 70 on the right side of the valley or the very quiet roads and tracks we prefer on the left.

Distance from Canterbury: 1011km **Distance to Rome:** 1065km

Ascent: 780m **Descent:** 362m

Way Point N°	Way Point Distance (metres)	Total Distance (kilometres)	Directions	Verification Point	Compass	Altitude (metres)
38.01	0	0.0	From the Tourist Office on rue de la Gare, turn left and proceed straight ahead through place Centrale	Follow signs for the Col Grand St Bernard	SW	475
38.02	400	0.4	Ahead, direction Grand St Bernard	Sculpture in middle of roundabout	SW	476
38.03	1000	1.4	Continue straight ahead direction Grand St Bernard	avenue du Grand Saint Bernard	SW	490
38.04	600	2.0	At roundabout straight ahead direction Grand St Bernard,	Pedestrian sign, direction Orsières on right	SW	497
38.05	300	2.3	Just before river bridge, turn left direction Orsières. - the pathway ahead is prohibited to horses and cyclists and involves narrow stretches with exposed falls on the right side. Alternate Route remains on the road and crosses the bridge	VF sign	S	500
38.06	120	2.4	Pass through the car park and turn left onto a flight of steps		S	507
38.07	800	3.2	Cross the railway and turn right	VF sign	S	534
38.08	400	3.6	Turn left after passing through a tunnel	VF sign	N	561
38.09	60	3.7	Turn sharp right to go up a flight of steps	VF sign	SE	569
38.10	400	4.1	Take left fork	Pèdestre sign	E	589

Martigny to Orsières 20.2 km

Way Point N°	Way Point Distance (metres)	Total Distance (kilometres)	Directions	Verification Point	Compass	Altitude (metres)
38.11	2300	6.4	Turn left and then sharp right over a small pedestrian bridge	River to the right, vines on left	SE	606
38.12	120	6.5	Continue straight ahead with the road bridge on right and river on left		E	611
38.13	300	6.8	Turn right to go under the road bridge	Pèdestre sign, rue Principale	NE	613
38.14	130	6.9	Turn left into Bovernier	Pèdestre sign	NE	616
38.15	300	7.2	At junction with main road turn right	Pèdestre sign, Small wooden garage on right	E	620
38.16	300	7.5	Turn right off the main road	Pèdestre sign, water trough	E	615
38.17	300	7.8	Turn right onto a grass track	Pèdestre sign	E	626
38.18	1900	9.7	Continue on the grass track	Pèdestre sign	E	678
38.19	2100	11,8	Turn left over a railway bridge and then bear right on rue de la Gravenne	Pèdestre sign	NE	726
38.20	500	12.3	Turn right in the centre of Sembrancher on rue Amédée IV	Pèdestre sign	SE	718
38.21	110	12.4	Turn right direction Grand St Bernard on rte du Cleusuit	Pèdestre sign - Orsières 3.6 hours	S	721
38.22	90	12.5	Turn left on chemin Gaspard-Etienne Delasoie. - Route 70 goes straight ahead keeping to the right side of the valley above and parallel to the railway rejoining our route at Way Point #33 at entry to Orsières		E	722

Way Point N°	Way Point Distance (metres)	Total Distance (kilometres)	Directions	Verification Point	Compass	Altitude (metres)
38.23	300	12.8	Proceed straight head across main road on rte des Moulins	Pèdestre sign	E	729
38.24	300	13.1	Turn right with barn on the right	Pèdestre sign	S	731
38.25	50	13.2	Turn right up the hill beside the barn	Pèdestre sign	S	737
38.26	300	13.5	Cross over minor road and continue on track. - for a more gentle ascent on tarmac bear right on the minor road to Chamoille d'Orsières – Way Point #29	Pèdestre sign	S	783
38.27	90	13.6	Keep to the right	Pèdestre sign	S	792
38.28	1900	15.5	The track joins a minor road, bear right direction Orsières	Pèdestre sign	SW	932
38.29	800	16.3	Turn left direction Orsières, rte des Prés Neufs	Pèdestre sign	S	910
38.30	500	16.8	Fork left on the road		S	938
38.31	1700	18.5	Descend to main road and turn left to follow main road	Direction Orsières	S	886
38.32	900	19.4	Turn right to leave main road	Direction Orsières	S	859
38.33	600	19.0	Fork left on chemin de Fleu		S	879
38.34	200	20.2	Arrive in Orsières (L) centre - place Centrale			892

Alternate Martigny to Orsières 5.0 km

This alternate route takes the main road passing through enclosed galleries and should the tackled with great care. Unfortunately it offers the only option for cyclists and horse-riders for the first sections of the climb from Martigny. A very early start should be considered to minimize the the level of traffic on the road.

Way Point N°	Way Point Distance (metres)	Total Distance (kilometres)	Directions	Compass	Altitude (metres)
1	0	0	Continue straight ahead across the river bridge	NW	504
2	70	0.1	Turn left on rue Principale	SW	501
3	600	0.7	At junction with main road, cross over and turn left. **Note:** take great care, heavy traffic and enclosed road galleries ahead	SE	516
4	2800	3.5	Turn right on slip road and follow rue Principale parallel to main road	E	617
5	1500	5.0	Rejoin main route at Waypoint #14 proceeding straight ahead into Bovernier		616

"It was high morning and everyone was full of fear and trembling. Through holy prayer we were preparing to face menacing death..." written by a Belgian abbot in 1129, just before beginning his ascent on the Great St Bernard Pass.

In Orsières, you will be poised to trace the most ancient route through the Western Alps: The Great St Bernard Pass, crossing at 2,473 metres and one of the highest of the Alpine frontier passes. Named after Saint Bernard of Menthon, who founded a hospice at its summit in the 11th century, The Grand-St-Bernard Pass has been in use since the Bronze Age - tribes and armies have tramped their way to and fro for millennia since. In 390 BC, a Gaulish army crossed to defeat Rome, and from the earliest times ordinary people used the pass to trade goods between northern Europe and Italy. Hannibal's famous crossing of the Alps in 217 BC is indelibly associated with the Grand-St-Bernard, and (though there's little actual evidence of it actually having taken place) in the 1930s the fabulously eccentric American travel writer, Richard Halliburton, rode his elephant over the pass to re-enact the journey. Sadly, the poor beast suffered from altitude sickness and stalled on the summit. So now it is your turn to see how far you get - good luck, listen out for the marmots, watch out for the weather and enjoy what could be the experience of a lifetime.

No matter how tough the climb, no matter how good or bad the weather, please ensure that you take time out to survey the towering mountains covered with ice as old as the earth and appreciate how much harder it must have been for the people who travelled all those thousands of years before. In 57 BC, Julius Caesar crossed the Summa Poenina (as it was known then) to conquer the pagan peoples of Martigny who worshipped the Celtic god Poenn (the chain of great peaks on the Swiss–Italian frontier is still called the Pennine Alps). Shortly after, Emperor Augustus built a road across the pass and left a temple to Jupiter on the summit, which subsequently lent its name to the area (Mons Iovis, or Mont Joux). Unfortunately the temple was sacked with the fall of Rome, but since the great and the good continued to tramp the road it is assumed that a refuge may well have remained on the pass. Pope Stephen II crossed in November 753 to meet with Pepin the Short (vertically challenged), King of France; while in 800 Charlemagne crossed back following his coronation in Milan. In the early 900s, Huns and Saracens swept through the region, raping, pillaging and destroying churches, so in an attempt to keep them quiet, Hugh of Provence, King of Italy, granted them guardianship of the Mont Joux pass, whereupon they just changed their

focus and terrorized travellers instead - a prototype for today's muggers. Deeply concerned by the disruption caused to merchants and pilgrims Europe-wide, King Canute of Denmark took King Rudolf III of Burgundy to one side to have a quiet word. As a result the heathens were ejected and the archdeacon of Aosta, one Bernard of Menthon (who had spent years tending to travellers coming down off the pass stripped of all their belongings), was given permission to oversee the construction of the hospice. Bernard himself travelled around the area, spreading the word of God and was beatified shortly after his death in the 1080s. Pope Pius XI confirmed him as patron saint of the Alps in 1923. The hospice immediately became a welcome point of safety on an extremely dangerous route, attracting favours and gifts from royal and noble households. Throughout the Middle Ages, the hospice provided free shelter and food to pilgrims, clerics and travellers, many crossing to and from Rome. By 1817 some 20,000 people were using the road annually. During the wars of the 1790s, entire armies crossed the pass and, in May 1800, Napoleon led 40,000 troops over the pass into Italy, consuming on the way 21,724 bottles of wine, a tonne and a half of cheese, 800kg of meat, and more. The bill with the hospice came to a staggering Fr.40,000 but Napoleon dodged payment. Fifty years later, the monks received Fr.18,500 towards the total, but had to wait until May 1984 for a token gesture of account settling (which included the construction of a swimming pool) from French president François Mitterrand. The hospice on the pass is still used by Augustinian monks who, with their St. Bernard dogs, provide services to travellers. When you finally reach the summit of the Great St Bernard Pass, the first building you will see is the Combe de Morte a 'charnel house' where the corpses of those who never made it over the pass were mummified by the cold, but don't worry it is no longer in use. Next look out for the sign informing travellers that they are 2473 metres up - an obligatory photo stop. Then head for the hostel or hotel and a much needed shower. After that, if you still have sufficient energy, visit the St. Bernard Dog Museum, which is also an important part of the Great St Bernard Pass history. Probably descended from mastiff-like dogs, the St Bernard dogs were brought to the hospice in the late 17th century and remained loyal companions to the monks living there. The name St. Bernard was dedicated to Bernard, the 11th century monk. The most famous dog was Barry, who reportedly saved somewhere between 40 and 100 lives. There is a monument to Barry in the Cimetiere des Chiens, and his body is preserved in the Natural History Museum in Berne.

Orsières to Great St. Bernard Pass Summit 24.9 km

Signs to Look Out For

Route Summary: the off-road route is generally a steady, but continuous climb to the summit with short steeper sections. The route bypasses the intermediate towns and so walkers need to be well prepared. Horse riders and mountain bikers can use parts of the route but will need to divert to avoid the steepest and narrowest sections. Options are provided for each group to leave the off-road route and join the on-road section. Be sure to check the weather before departure.

Distance from Canterbury: 1031km **Distance to Rome:** 1045km

Ascent: 1806m **Descent:** 220m

Way Point N°	Way Point Distance (metres)	Total Distance (kilometres)	Directions	Verification Point	Compass	Altitude (metres)
39.01	0	0.0	From the place Centrale with the Hotel des Alpes behind, bear right	rue de la Commune	S	891
39.02	80	0.1	Bear right onto Charrière Challant	Avoid ruelle de la Montoz	SW	894
39.03	100	0.2	Turn left on route de Podemainge	VF sign	S	892
39.04	60	0.2	Bear left and then immediately right on place de la Creuse	VF sign	SW	895
39.05	200	0.4	At a small crossroads, go straight ahead, direction Liddes	Route de la Podemainge	S	894
39.06	200	0.6	Stay on tarmac road and bear right	Pedestrian sign	S	906
39.07	300	0.9	Continue straight ahead	VF and pedestrian sign and house on right	S	918
39.08	200	1.1	Turn right to cross over bridge	VF sign and RP1993 on bridge	S	934
39.09	80	1.2	Bear right up hill	VF and pedestrian sign	W	936
39.10	300	1.5	Bear left up hill following the Route 70 signs		SE	956
39.11	2500	4.0	At fork above Fornex bear right. - bike riders may prefer to bear left on the roadway for an easy descent to the river crossing at Waypoint #15		SE	1206

Orsières to Great St. Bernard Pass Summit 24.9 km

Way Point N°	Way Point Distance (metres)	Total Distance (kilometres)	Directions	Verification Point	Compass	Altitude (metres)
39.12	110	4.1	At fork bear right to pass between houses in Fornex		SE	1207
39.13	200	4.3	Bear left down the hill towards the woods on a narrow track in the direction of Les Moulins. - Route 70 turns to the right and takes the higher path through the forest returning beside Way Point #16		SE	1209
39.14	400	4.7	As track emerges onto road turn right towards the river		E	1131
39.15	60	4.8	Cross the bridge, turn right direction Liddes. - the track ahead is extremely difficult for horse and bike riders who should turn left and climb the hill to join the On-road Route at Waypoint #3	Follow narrowing path with river on the right	S	1131
39.16	1400	6.2	Narrow track intersects with broad track, turn right to cross river and then left on track through woods	River on the left	SE	1238
39.17	700	6.9	On junction with broad track turn left towards the village of Dranse		SE	1234
39.18	300	7.2	At T-junction turn right towards village. - turn left on Route 70 to visit Liddes and follow the upper route to Bourg-Saint-Pierre or join the On-road Route		SW	1253
39.19	90	7.3	In Dranse bear left		SE	1260

Way Point N°	Way Point Distance (metres)	Total Distance (kilometres)	Directions	Verification Point	Compass	Altitude (metres)
39.20	130	7.4	Straight ahead	Track narrows with river to the left	SE	1268
39.21	900	8.3	Bear left to skirt reservoir and water plant		E	1324
39.22	170	8.5	Turn right to continue around reservoir		SE	1332
39.23	150	8.6	Turn right across the bridge		SW	1329
39.24	60	8.7	After crossing bridge turn left to follow the river	River to the left	S	1333
39.25	3500	12.2	At junction with broad track turn sharp right. - to visit Bourg-Saint-Pierre (XLIX) on the Alternate Route or rejoin the On-road Route, turn left		N	1524
39.26	130	12.3	Turn left direction Barrage des Toules	VF sign	S	1536
39.27	1400	13.7	Straight ahead direction Lac des Toules	VF sign	S	1607
39.28	700	14,4	Bear left down the hill	VF sign	S	1701
39.29	300	14,7	Continue straight ahead with the river on the left	VF sign	SW	1681
39.30	300	15.0	Turn left of the house and then through small wicket gate onto a narrow grass track	VF sign	SW	1711
39.31	400	15.4	At the time of writing there were major civil engineering works taking place ahead and it was necessary to bear right on the steep track up the hill following the pedestrian signs and then turn right and then left on the gravel track to skirt the dam and bypass the next Way Point		SW	1723

Orsières to Great St. Bernard Pass Summit 24.9 km

Way Point N°	Way Point Distance (metres)	Total Distance (kilometres)	Directions	Verification Point	Compass	Altitude (metres)
39.32	200	15.2	Turn right onto the gravel track	VF sign	SW	1767
39.33	400	15.6	Fork left with reservoir on the left	VF sign	SW	1824
39.34	800	16.4	Continue straight ahead on small track downhill towards the water.	Do not follow track up the hill	S	1836
39.35	2500	18.9	Straight ahead direction Col St Bernard and the chemin Historique sign. Ahead the route is often blocked by cattle fencing. Horse riders can turn left here over the wooden bridge to regain the road route at the upper end of the avalanche gallery	VF sign	SW	1896
39.36	800	19.7	Straight ahead direction Col St Bernard		SW	1987
39.37	400	20.1	Bear left towards farm buildings		SW	2053
39.38	150	20.3	Turn left beside farm buildings to follow valley in the direction of the road		SE	2039
39.39	600	20.9	Turn left towards the road		NE	2027
39.40	80	20.9	Turn right onto a path running parallel to the road		S	2035
39.41	800	21.7	Cross straight over the road. - even in summer there is often snow and ice on the pathway ahead		SW	2106
39.42	3200	24.9	Arrive at col Grand St Bernard summit			2477

Alternate route by road from Orsières to the col Grand-Saint-Bernard summit 25.7km This alternate route takes the main road passing through enclosed galleries and should be tackled with great care. An early start should be considered to minimize the the level of traffic on the road below the tunnel entrance. The route may be preferred in difficult weather conditions and has the advantage of easy access to more points of shelter

Way Point N°	Way Point Distance (metres)	Total Distance (kilometres)	Directions	Verification Point	Compass	Altitude (metres)
1	0	0.0	From the place Centrale with the Hôtel des Alpes behind bear left on the main exit road towards the col	rue de Grand Saint Bernard	S	891
2	600	0.6	Continue straight ahead under the road bridges to join the main road and continue climbing		SE	930
3	4200	4.8	On the crown of the bend just after passing Fontaine-Dessous, walkers and riders can join here from the Off-road Route. Continue straight ahead	Road joins from the right	SE	1184
4	6400	11.2	Continue straight ahead. **Note:** at the entrance to gallery, cyclists continue straight ahead, horse riders and walkers can bear right onto a small track and then bear left crossing over the gallery and rejoining the road beyond the gallery end.		S	1524
5	1500	12.7	For the summit cyclists continue straight ahead on the road. **Note:** to visit Bourg Saint Pierre (XLIX) or for horse riders and walkers to avoid the 4km gallery ahead bear right into the town and join the Alternate Route		S	1606
6	1400	14.1	Straight ahead at entry to avalanche gallery		S	1689
7	5000	19.1	Bear right to leave gallery before the tunnel entrance		S	1919
8	2500	21.6	Walking route crosses from the right		SW	2104
9	4100	25.7	Arrive at the summit of the col Grand Saint Bernard	Hospice to the left		2477

Alternate route to visit Bourg Saint Pierre 2.5 km

Alternate route provides access to Bourg-Saint-Pierre from the Dranze river-side.

Way Point N°	Way Point Distance (metres)	Total Distance (kilometres)	Directions	Verification Point	Compass	Altitude (metres)
1	0	0.0	From Way Point #25 on the main route turn left, cross the valley bottom and climb the the hill towards the town		SE	1520
2	1500	1.5	At the T-junction, turn right into the town		S	1624
3	200	1.7	Bear right on rte Principale. **Note:** Route 70 continues straight ahead rejoining the main route at Way Point #32. However, at the time of writing there were major engineering works around Lac des Toules blocking the Route 70 track	Close beside the chucrh	S	1632
4	100	1.8	Bear right on the track towards the valley bottom		SW	1633
5	700	2.5	Rejoin the Off-road Route, climbing the hill and turning towards the dam - Way Point #27			1606

Useful Contacts

Tourist/Information Offices

Office du Tourisme 1945 BOURG-ST-PIERRE bourg-st-pierre@st-bernard.ch

B&B/Hotel	Price
Auberge des Charmettes - 1946 BOURG-ST-PIERRE Tel: 41 (0)27 787 11 50 (Dormitory) gtornare@swissonline.ch	B1
Auberge du Vieux-Moulin - 1946 BOURG-ST-PIERRE Tel: 41 41 (0)27 787 11 69	B2
Au Petit Velan - 1946 BOURG ST PIERRE Tel: 0041 (0)27 787 11 41 rjoris@petit-velan.ch	
Au Bivouac de Napoleon - 1946 BOURG ST PIERRE Tel: 0041 (0)27 787 11 62 bivouac.napoleon@st-bernard.ch	B2
Le Mont-Joux - 1946 BOURG ST PIERRE Tel: 0041 (0)27 787 11 66 bivouac.napoleon@st-bernard.ch	B2
Hôtel du Grand St Bernard, rte de Gd St Bernard - 1945 LIDDES Tel: 0041 (0)27 783 13 02	B2
Hostel	**Price**
PR Maison St Pierre - 1946 BOURG-ST-PIERRE Tel: 0041 (0)79 823 84 16 www.maisonstpierre.ch	B1
Camping	**Price**
Camping du Grand Saint Bernard - 1946 BOURG SAINT PIERRE Tel: 41 (0)27 787 14 11 reservation@campinggrand-st-bernard.ch	B1
Religious Hostel	**Price**
Paroisse Catholic BOURG ST PIERRE, Contact: Girard Jean-Michel Tel: 41 (0)27 783 11 44 Mobile: (0)79 414 98 17 paroisse@orsieres.com	Donation
Hospice du Gd-St-Bernard, Col du Grand-St-Bernard - 1946 GRAND ST BERNARD Tel: 41 (0)27 787 12 36 hospicestbernard@gsbernard.ch	B2

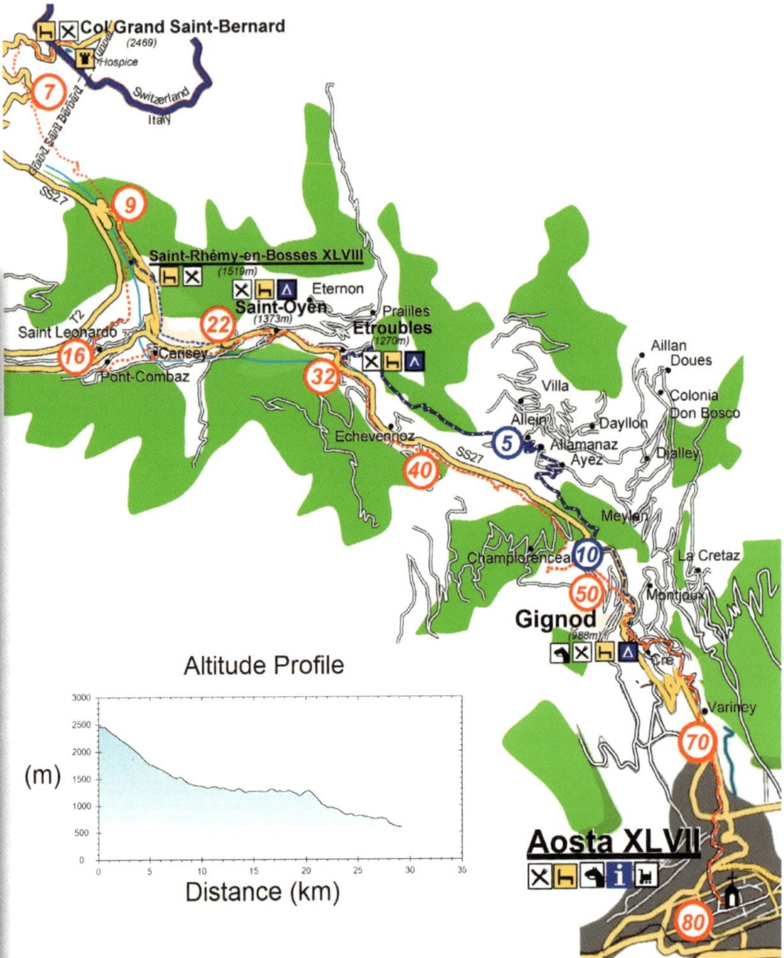

Route Summary: the descent to Aosta is generally gentle and progressive on off-road track. There are a number of opportunities to break the journey. Horse and bike riders should be prepared to take Alternate Route #2.

Distance from Canterbury: 1056km **Distance to Rome::** 1020km

Ascent: 371m **Descent:** 1881m

Way Point N°	Way Point Distance (metres)	Total Distance (kilometres)	Directions	Verification Point	Compass	Altitude (metres)
40.01	0	0.0	With the hostel behind continue straight ahead down the hill towards the border post.		W	2469
40.02	500	0.5	At the Italian border post bear right on the path	Pass beside the hotel	W	2450
40.03	150	0.7	Go straight ahead beside the statue of Saint Bernard		W	2459
40.04	300	0.8	Just before the avalanche gallery cross the road to join a track at the foot of a stone slope	Yellow Arrow	W	2419
40.05	400	1.2	Fork left following yellow arrows	Yellow Arrow	S	2362
40.06	700	1.9	Cross straight over the road and continue on track	Yellow Arrow	SE	2270
40.07	500	2.4	Cross over road onto grass track	Path No. 13	S	2207
40.08	500	2.9	Fork right down the hill	Yellow Arrow	SE	2133
40.09	2700	5.6	Turn left onto road SS27	Yellow Arrow	S	1715
40.10	300	5.9	Turn right onto small track and then left in the direction of Saint-Rhemy	VF sign	SE	1688
40.11	400	6.3	Enter Saint-Rhemy-en-Bosses (XLVIII) and continue straight ahead down the hill on the road	Frazione Cerisey	S	1635
40.12	190	6.5	At the fork at the end of the main street turn right over the bridge and then left. **Note:** for the alternate and shorter (by 1.5km) route bear left up the hill	River on the left after crossing the bridge	S	1614

Great St. Bernard Pass Summit to Aosta 29.0 km

Way Point N°	Way Point Distance (metres)	Total Distance (kilometres)	Directions	Verification Point	Compass	Altitude (metres)
40.13	1300	7.8	At the end of the track bear right on the road		W	1509
40.14	110	7.9	On entering San Leonardo keep left at the first junction		S	1530
40.15	130	8.0	At the crossroads go straight ahead down the hill	Frazione Predumaz Falcoz	SW	1522
40.16	300	8.3	Cross the main road and continue straight ahead down the hill		S	1507
40.17	80	8.4	Cross the road – Frazione Saint Leonard – and continue straight ahead	Chiesa di Saint Leonard	E	1473
40.18	700	9.1	At the T-junction with the road – Frazione Cerisey – turn right		SE	1393
40.19	200	9.3	At the exit from Cerisey turn left	Before the bridge	E	1380
40.20	500	9.8	Continue straight ahead through fields		E	1363
40.21	900	10.7	On approaching the quiet rue de la Montée bear left up hill on the track towards the main road		NE	1320
40.22	300	11.0	Turn right onto the SS27 via Roma into the village of Saint-Oyen. **Note:** the alternate route joins from the left	Sign for Martigny-Aosta	E	1354
40.23	500	11.5	Turn right off the main road onto via Verraz	Sign for Martigny-Aosta	SW	1344
40.24	80	11.6	Turn left down the hill between houses	Sign for Martigny-Aosta	S	1333
40.25	70	11.7	At T-junction turn left on Strada di Flassin		E	1320

Way Point N°	Way Point Distance (metres)	Total Distance (kilometres)	Directions	Verification Point	Compass	Altitude (metres)
40.26	400	12.1	At the junction with the main road, cross over and take the turning to the right running very close to the main road	The road quickly deteriorates into a track	SE	1326
40.27	800	12.9	On approaching Etroubles cross the minor road rue de Vachèry and follow the pathway towards the town centre		E	1275
40.28	100	12.0	Rejoin the main road and continue straight ahead on the pavement		SE	1272
40.29	110	13.1	On the apex of the bend bear left leaving the main road to follow the minor road into Etroubles		SE	1268
40.30	80	13.2	At the crossroads turn right. **Note:** the track ahead becomes very narrow between a fast running aqueduct and steep hill-sides. Horse-riders are advised to go straight ahead and follow the alternate route to Gignod. Bike riders can take the main road to the left at the next Way Point	Rue du Mont Velan	SW	1266
40.31	130	13.3	Cross the river and the SS27and bear right		S	1279
40.32	80	13.2	Turn left in front of the restaurant on rue Saint-Roch	Sign for Martigny-Aosta,	E	1292
40.33	80	13.4	Turn right onto an unmade road		SE	1301
40.34	800	14.2	Turn right onto the main road	VF sign	S	1237
40.35	300	14.5	Turn right onto a grassy track	VF sign	SE	1250
40.36	500	14.0	Turn right onto road in Echevennoz	VF sign, farm on right	SE	1267

Great St. Bernard Pass Summit to Aosta 29.0 km

Way Point N°	Way Point Distance (metres)	Total Distance (kilometres)	Directions	Verification Point	Compass	Altitude (metres)
40.37	150	15.1	Walkers turn right onto track	VF sign and sign for Martigny-Aosta	E	1263
40.38	600	15.7	Turn right onto road	VF sign	E	1256
40.39	60	15.8	Turn right to proceed between two houses	VF sign	E	1257
40.40	20	15.8	Turn left on track	VF sign	S	1258
40.41	70	15.9	Bear left alongside the aqueduct	VF sign, concrete water trough	SE	1277
40.42	1200	17.1	Fork left down the hill	VF sign	E	1284
40.43	60	17.1	Fork right back up the hill	VF sign	SE	1271
40.44	300	17.4	Fork left down hill	VF sign	SE	1245
40.45	1500	18.9	Turn right onto a road and then immediately left to get back on the track slightly up the hill	VF sign	S	1242
40.46	800	19.7	Take the left fork	VF sign	SE	1184
40.47	900	20.6	Turn left on the track	VF signs, Martigny-Aosta signs	SE	1219
40.48	200	20.8	Remain on grass track	Ignore the dirt track that goes off to the right	SE	1176
40.49	500	21.3	Cross over the road to continue down the hill on the grass track	VF sign	SE	1079
40.50	60	21.4	Sharp left down the hill	VF sign	E	1065
40.51	90	21.5	Straight ahead on long flight of steps.		SE	1036
40.52	50	21.5	Turn right onto the road and proceed down the hill	VF sign	SE	1025
40.53	30	21.6	Almost immediately turn left back onto the grass track	VF sign	SE	1020

Way Point N°	Way Point Distance (metres)	Total Distance (kilometres)	Directions	Verification Point	Compass	Altitude (metres)
40.54	80	21.6	Turn left onto the road to proceed down the hill on Frazione Lexert	VF sign	SE	1009
40.55	60	21.7	Turn left to proceed down a small grass track	VF sign	SE	998
40.56	60	21.8	Turn left back down onto the road and then immediately right between the houses	VF sign	SE	993
40.57	200	21.9	Turn right down the hill		W	960
40.58	80	22.0	Turn left to go down the hill and against the traffic		SW	957
40.59	60	22.1	Turn right at junction with main road. **Note:** alternate routes merge here		S	949
40.60	200	22.3	Arrive Gignod, continue straight ahead on the main road	Camp site Europa on the left	S	948
40.61	120	22.4	Turn left direction Martigny-Aosta	TAM Martigny-Aosta)	SE	949
40.62	500	22.9	Turn sharp left downhill on a smaller road	TAM sign Martigny-Aosta	NE	900
40.63	300	23.2	Turn sharp right downhill – Frazione Chez Henry	VF sign	SE	868
40.64	500	23.7	Turn left onto tarmac road and then immediately right	VF sign	SE	817
40.65	500	24.2	Turn left at the top of the hill	VF sign	SE	806
40.66	400	24.6	Turn right on Frazione Chez Roncoz	VF sign	S	758
40.67	600	25.2	Bear left down the hill on Frazione Variney	Parallel to main road	S	780
40.68	110	25.3	Bear left onto a smaller road	VF sign	SE	772

Great St. Bernard Pass Summit to Aosta 29.0 km

Way Point N°	Way Point Distance (metres)	Total Distance (kilometres)	Directions	Verification Point	Compass	Altitude (metres)
40.69	400	25.7	At T-junction with main road turn left and remain on a small grass track which just skirts the outside of the barrier	VF sign	S	757
40.70	200	25.9	Track rejoins the main road continue downhill	VF sign	S	741
40.71	800	26.7	Fork right uphill. **Note:** to avoid numerous obstacles, cyclists and horse-riders should remain on the main road until the roundabout at Way Point #79	Signs for Martigny-Aosta and VF sign	S	710
40.72	180	26.9	Fork left on reaching the top of a small rise	VF sign	S	719
40.73	300	27.2	Fork left onto unmade road	VF sign	S	730
40.74	80	27.3	Turn sharp left downhill		SE	722
40.75	90	27.4	Turn right onto road and proceed up the hill	VF sign	SW	699
40.76	180	27.6	Turn left across the road and bear left down a grassy track	VF sign	S	689
40.77	400	27.9	Cross straight over the road and continue down the track	VF sign	S	646
40.78	120	28.1	At T-junction turn right onto the road and proceed down the hill	VF sign	SW	631
40.79	400	28.5	At the roundabout take the pedestrian crossing and continue into the centre of Aosta	VF sign	SE	596
40.80	200	28.7	Proceed straight into pedestrian zone		S	590
40.81	200	28.9	In piazza Roncas turn left and immediately right into the narrow street towards the Cathedral		E	583

Way Point N°	Way Point Distance (metres)	Total Distance (kilometres)	Directions	Verification Point	Compass	Altitude (metres)
40.82	70	28.9	Turn right on via Forum		SE	582
40.83	70	29.0	Arrive in piazza della Cattedrale/piazza Giovanni XXIII			580

Alternate #1 Note: After leaving Saint-Rhemy the route takes a direct but sometimes narrow path to Saint-Oyen bypassing San Leonardo. The route reduces total distance by 1.5km.

Way Point N°	Way Point Distance (metres)	Total Distance (kilometres)	Directions	Verification Point	Compass	Altitude (metres)
1	0	0.0	Turn left up the hill to rejoin the SS27	Frazione Cerisey	SE	1619
2	60	0.1	At intersection with SS27 turn left		SE	1611
3	300	0.4	At apex of hairpin turn right on track direction Aosta		S	1634
4	700	1.1	Fork right on track		SE	1684
5	1500	2.6	Track intersects with SS27. Cross over and turn left on the other side.		E	1359
6	300	2.9	Rejoin the main route at Way Point #22	Sign for Martigny-Aosta		1350

Alternate #2 Great St. Bernard Pass Summit to Aosta 11.1 km

The alternate route avoids a narrow pathway trapped between an aqueduct and steep hillsides with steps that are impassable by horses. The alternate route follows small roads on the east side of the river before crossing the valley floor and climbing to rejoin the main route on the entry to Gignod.

Way Point N°	Way Point Distance (metres)	Total Distance (kilometres)	Directions	Verification Point	Compass	Altitude (metres)
1	0	0.0	At the crossroads turn left on rue du Mont Velan		NE	1266
2	90	0.1	Take the fourth turning on the right rte Millet		SE	1272
3	80	0.2	Turn left on rue du Bordonnet		NE	1273
4	150	0.3	At the T-junction turn right on rue de Vachèry direction Allein		SE	1302
5	4800	5.1	On approaching Allein turn right on Frazione Clavel		SE	1221
6	400	5.5	At T-junction turn left and continue down the hill through a series of bends	Frazione Frein	SE	1179
7	700	6.2	Bear left on Frazione Ayez		SE	1155
8	500	6.7	At the T-junction turn right on Frazione Ayez		W	1067
9	200	6.9	At the T-junction turn left continuing on Frazione Ayez	Descend to valley floor then climb hill towards main road	SE	1064
10	2200	9.1	At the T-junction turn left on the main road into Gignod		SE	1111
11	2000	11.1	Rejoin main route in Gignod at Way Point #59 and continue on the main road			948

Hotel/B&B - large choice of hotels in Aosta	**Price**
Hotel Des Alpes, 15, Località Cuchepache - 11010 SAINT-RHÉMY-EN-BOSSES Tel: 0039 (0)165 780 916	B3
Mont Velan 13, 14, rue Grand Saint Bernard - SAINT OYEN 11010 Tel: 0039 (0)165 78 524 hotel@montvelan.it	B3
PR Château Verdun, 3, rue de Flassin - 11010 SAINT OYEN Tel: 0039 (0)165 78247 casagsb@gsbernard.ch	B2
Dortoir Ostello Echevennoz - 11014 ETROUBLES Tel: 0039 (0)16578225 ruffierdidier@libero.it	B1
Lo Chalet, 10, Fraz. Fiou - 11010 GIGNOD Mobile: 0039 347 1599705 barnabo54@virgilio.it www.bedandbreakfastineurope.com/lochalet	B2
Agriturismo Le Couis Di Margueret Ivana - 11010 GIGNOD Tel: 0039 (0)165 56119	B2
Agriturismo Le Myosotis Di Blanc Maria Luisa, 7, Localita Arlio D7 - 11010 GI-GNOD Tel: 0039 (0)165 256893	B2
Hotel Papa Grand, Loc. Variney - 11010 GIGNOD Tel: 0039 (0)165 56076	B2
Focolare S. Giuseppe, 36, via S. Xavier De Mais - 11100 AOSTA Tel: 0039 (0)165 262089	B2
Borrano, 9, via Voison 11100 AOSTA Tel: 0039 (0)165 43224	B2
La Roche, 110/a località Signayes, fraz Clou - 11100 AOSTA Tel: 0039 (0)165 262 426 info@laroche.it www.laroche.it	B2

Accommodation in Religious Houses	**Price**
Cure de Saint-Rhemy - 11010 SAINT-RHÉMY-EN-BOSSES Mobile: 0039 333 6816012	B1
Parrocchia Saint Martin, 179, Corso St Martin - 11100 AOSTA Tel: 0039 (0)165 553373	Donation
Parrocchia Saint Ansemlo, Corso Ivrea - 11100 AOSTA Tel: 0039 (0)165 40627	Donation
Focolare S. Guiseppe, 36, via S. Xavier De Maistre - 11100 AOSTA Tel: 0039 (0)165 262089	Donation

Camping	**Price**
Del Mulino, Loc. Flassin - 11010 SAINT OYEN Tel: 0039 (0)165 78119 info@gransanbernardo.net www.campeggiodelmulino.it	
Camping Tunnel, 4, str Chevrieres - 11014 ETROUBLES Tel: 0039 (0)165-78292 info@campingtunnel.it www.campingtunnel.it	B1
PR Camping Europa, Loc. Plan Chateau - 11010 GIGNOD Tel: 0039 (0)165 56444 **Note:** Also takes horses	B1

Aosta Town Map

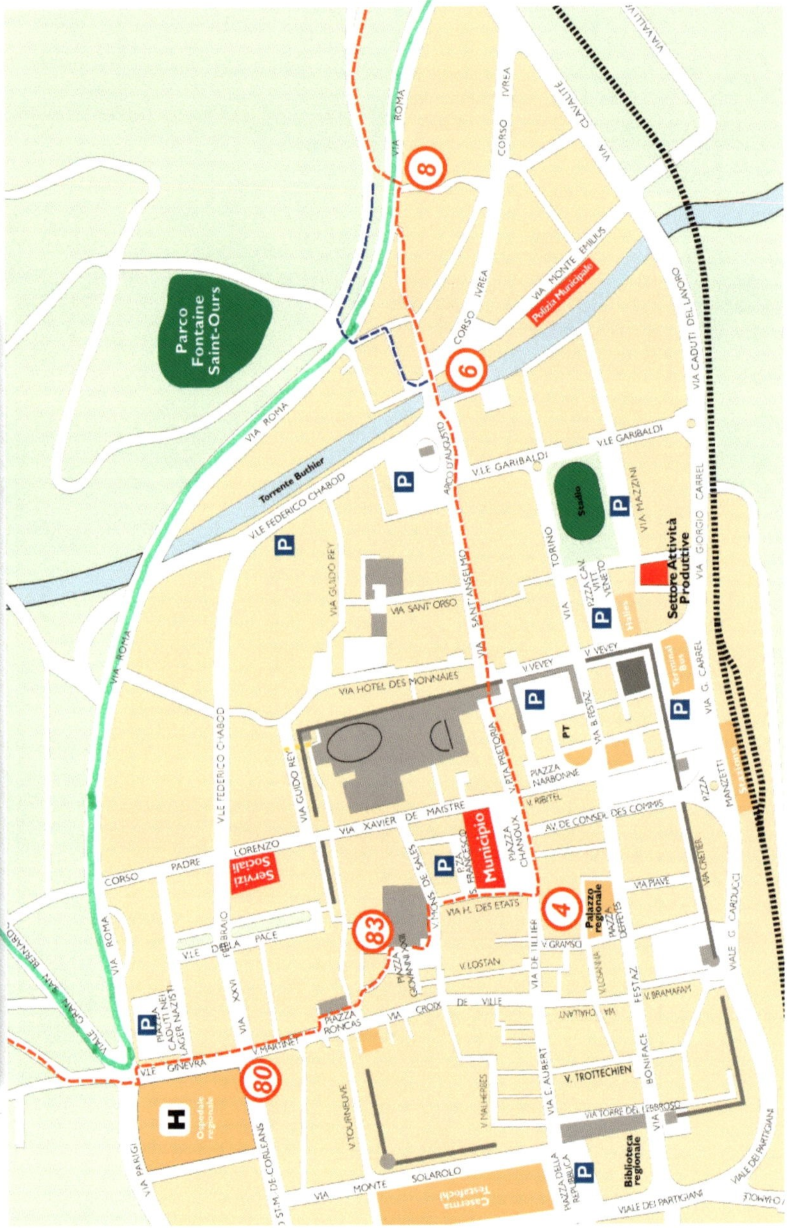

Hotel/B&B	Price
Hotel Cuney, 36, Loc. Lignan - 11020 NUS Tel: 0039 (0)165 770 023 marisagrun@libero.it	B2
Le Bonheur, 53/a, Frazione Chez Croiset - 11020 FENIS Tel: 0039 (0)165 764117 www.agriturismo-lebonheur.com	B2
DEI CASTAGNETI 15, Localita Lassolaz - 11024 PONTEY Tel: 0039 (0)166 30 145 Takes horses	B2
Cave du Chateau 6, Localita Ussel - 11024 CHATILLON Tel: 0039 (0)166 61 352	B2
Hotel Dufour di Pession Alina, 16, v. Tollein - 11024 CHATILLON Tel: 0039 (0)166 61467 dufourtaxi@virgilio.it	B2
Clair Matin, 40, via Tour de Grange - 11024 CHATILLON Tel: 0039 (0)166 61822 daniela.vesan@email.it	B2

Religious Hostel	Price
Parrocchia Saint-Barthélemy, via Don A. Pramotton Prieur - 11020 NUS Tel: 0039 (0)165 767901	Donation

Camping	Price
Camping Dalai Lama, Loc. Promiod - 11024 - CHATILLON Mobile: 0039 335 6794563 www.campingdalailama.com info@dalailamavillage.it	B1

Equestrian

A.R.T.E. Attacchi, 53, Frazione Chez Croiset - 11020 FÉNIS info@arteattacchi.it
next to Le Bonheur and highly recommended (see blog)

Aosta, regional capital in the Aosta Valley, is rich in history. Traces of the ancient Augusta Pretoria (the Latin name) can be seen in the great Arch of Augustus (25 BC) and the remains of the Roman theatre. For Aosta the Middle Ages were anything but dark. As an important centre for commercial traffic between France and Switzerland, the city enjoyed a long period of prosperity. It is no coincidence that the Cathedral and Cathedral Church of S. Orso, two churches of great beauty, date back to the Middle Ages.

Useful Contacts

Tourist/Information Offices

Azienda Di Informazione E Accoglienza Turistica, 13, Route nationale du gd. St. Bernard - 11014 ETROUBLES Tel: 0039 (0)165 78568
www.gransanbernardo-valpelline.it

Azienda Di Informazione E Accoglienza Turistica, 2, piazza Chanoux - 11100 AOSTA
Tel: 0039 (0)165236627 uit-aosta@regione.vda.it

Doctor

Farcoz Dr. Rodolfo, 7, Localita' Arliod - 11010 GIGNOD Tel: 0039 (0)165 56220

VEGLIO DR. STEFANO, 46, vl. Pace - 11100 AOSTA Tel: 0039 (0)165 56463

Aosta to Chatillon 30.3 km

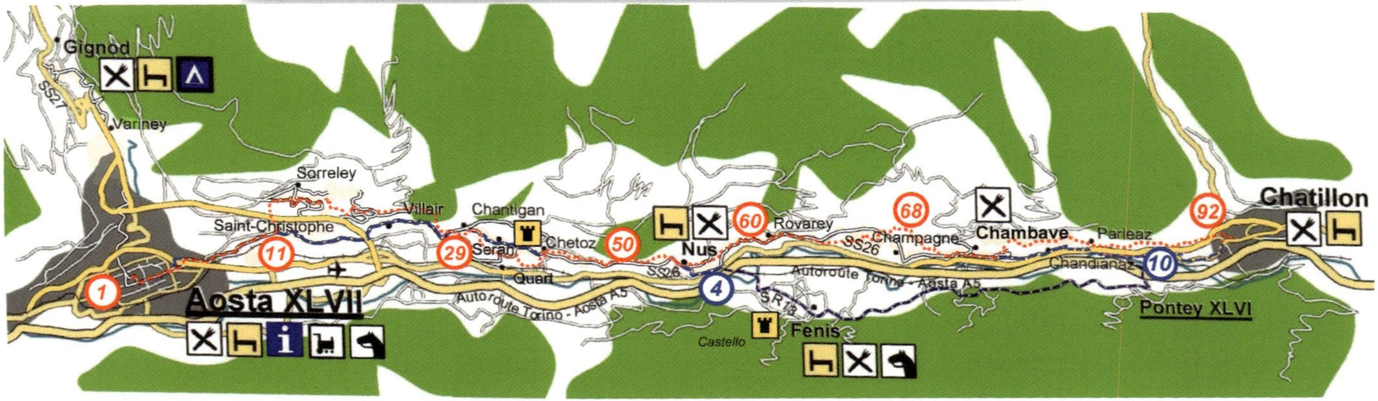

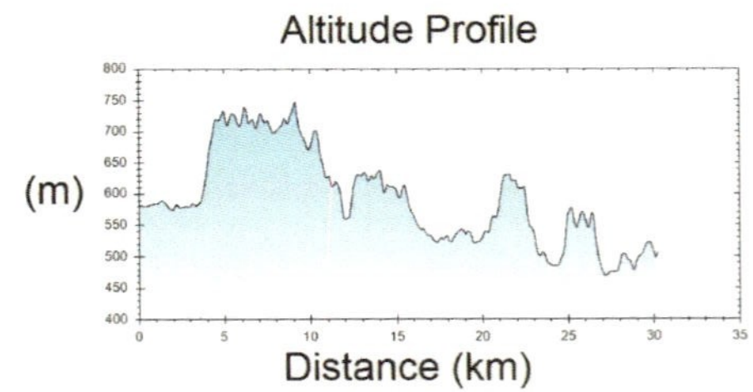

Route Summary: this is a long section where the official route involves strenuous off-road climbs and descents. The Alternates take generally very quiet tarmac routes.

Distance from Canterbury: 1085km **Distance to Rome:** 991km

Ascent: 900m **Descent:** 976m

Way Point N°	Way Point Distance (metres)	Total Distance (kilometres)	Directions	Verification Point	Compass	Altitude (metres)
41.01	0	0.0	Cross piazza della Cattedrale/piazza Giovanni XXIII		E	580
41.02	50	0.1	Turn left on via Monseigneur de Sales in piazza Chanoux		E	580
41.03	110	0.2	Turn right on via Hotel des Etats		SE	582
41.04	150	0.3	Turn left towards the Porta Pretoria	Beside Hotel de Ville	NE	579
41.05	700	1.0	At the roundabout at the end of the pedestrian zone proceed straight ahead and cross the bridge		E	584
41.06	140	1.1	At traffic lights continue straight ahead. **Note:** there is a flight of steps ahead – riders should turn left and follow via Mont-Velan, turn left on via Mont-Gelé, take the underpass under the busy ring-road and then turn right on via Scuola Militare Alpina	Follow signs for Hôpital Beauregard	E	586
41.07	90	1.2	Continue straight ahead on via Mont-Zerbion		E	587
41.08	200	1.4	Turn right then left mounting the steps and crossing the ring-road before following the road to the right and parallel to the ring road	Via Scuola Militare Alpina	E	589
41.09	170	1.6	Bear right on via Luigi Vaccari	VF sign	E	578
41.10	2000	3.6	Take the left fork Località Chaussod	VF sign	E	582

Way Point N°	Way Point Distance (metres)	Total Distance (kilometres)	Directions	Verification Point	Compass	Altitude (metres)
41.11	150	3.8	Bear left on the narrow lane in the direction Chiesa di Saint Christophe. **Note:** to reduce total distance by 1.6km and eliminate a number of steep climbs over difficult terrain keep right on Alternate Route #1	Località Chef-Lieu	NE	586
41.12	130	3.9	After passing beside the church take the steps to the left		NW	598
41.13	100	3.0	Cross the road and continue straight ahead up the steep hill		NW	613
41.14	200	4.2	Cross the main road and continue straight ahead on the footpath		N	658
41.15	130	4.3	At the crossroads continue straight ahead on the track		N	679
41.16	300	4.6	At the top of the hill turn right on the tarmac road		E	722
41.17	800	5.4	Turn left and then immediately right	Enter Sorreley	E	724
41.18	500	5.9	Continue straight ahead	Ignore turning to the left	E	712
41.19	500	6.4	Cross the stream		S	749
41.20	200	6.6	Cross over a track and continue ahead	Direction Castello di Quart	E	709
41.21	800	7.4	Cross a tarmac road and continue ahead on the track		E	730
41.22	600	8.0	The track becomes a path, and after a short descent take a clear path on the left		E	704
41.23	800	8.8	Continue straight ahead ignoring the turning to the right	Uphill	NE	712

Way Point N°	Way Point Distance (metres)	Total Distance (kilometres)	Directions	Verification Point	Compass	Altitude (metres)
41.24	70	8.9	Turn right on a tarmac road towards the Castello di Quart		SE	733
41.25	200	9.1	On the apex of the hairpin bend bear left towards the Castello		E	702
41.26	200	9.3	At the T-junction turn left	Beside the Castello	N	719
41.27	30	9.3	Avoid the turning to the left and continue straight ahead	Behind the Castello	SE	729
41.28	700	10.0	At a crossroads turn left on the track and immediately after turn right at the T-junction with the tarmac road		E	695
41.29	200	10.2	At the Stop sign bear right on the path. Alternate Route #1 joins from the road on the right	Downhill	SE	683
41.30	150	10.4	At the junction with a tarmac road turn left	Parallel to motorway below	E	667
41.31	120	10.5	Continue straight ahead	The road deteriorates into a path	NE	673
41.32	200	10.7	After a brief climb at a junction with a tarmac road bear right		SE	700
41.33	300	10.0	At the crossroads turn right and then immediately left. **Note:** to reduce the route by 800m and eliminate an unnecessary climb continue straight ahead through the village of Seran to Way Point #45 at Chetoz		SE	697
41.34	700	11.7	As the track bends to the left to climb the hill bear right on a small path	The path quickly turns right in the direction of the motorway	SE	625

Way Point N°	Way Point Distance (metres)	Total Distance (kilometres)	Directions	Verification Point	Compass	Altitude (metres)
41.35	200	11.9	After steep descent turn left at the intersection with the broad track		E	602
41.36	300	12.2	At the T-junction turn right	Downhill	SE	617
41.37	200	12.4	Near a fence turn left beside a stone wall. Beside an isolated tree take a path between two walls		E	570
41.38	190	12.6	At the T-junction turn right		SE	567
41.39	70	12.7	Take the left fork		E	558
41.40	130	12.8	At the fork at the end of the track, before reaching the road, take the steep path to the left		N	563
41.41	80	12.9	Continue straight ahead across the track	Uphill towards the forest	N	585
41.42	80	12,9	Continue straight ahead	Skirting the clearing	NE	606
41.43	110	13.1	Turn left along a track and then a tarmac road	Frazione Chetoz	N	613
41.44	80	13.1	At the next junction turn left on the tarmac road	Uphill	W	627
41.45	70	13.2	At the T-junction turn right. **Note:** the Alternate Route joins from the left	Towards chiesa di Diemoz	E	629
41.46	900	14.1	Take the right fork		E	635
41.47	600	14.7	At the end of the track take the faint pathway	Downhill and bearing left parallel to the motorway	E	621
41.48	200	14.9	Cross over a water-course		E	616
41.49	150	15.1	Continue straight ahead		E	609
41.50	300	15.3	Continue straight ahead	Avoid turning to the right	E	608
41.51	700	16.1	At a fork take the path to the right		E	612

Way Point N°	Way Point Distance (metres)	Total Distance (kilometres)	Directions	Verification Point	Compass	Altitude (metres)
41.52	200	16.3	At the end of the steep path turn left on the road and cross the bridge		SE	576
41.53	200	16.4	Continue straight ahead on the main road		E	566
41.54	150	16.6	Turn left. **Note:** to visit Pontey (XLVI), Nus and Fenis with its impressive castle bear right on Alternate Route #2	Via Pramatton	E	559
41.55	400	17.0	Continue straight ahead	Beside church	NE	539
41.56	160	17.2	Beside the monument turn right and then immediately left on the track		E	545
41.57	300	17.5	At the fork bear left downhill		NE	530
41.58	200	17.7	At the road junction turn right and then immediately left	Frazione Plantayes, towards Rovarey	NE	524
41.59	500	18.2	Continue straight ahead	Chateau on right	E	527
41.60	800	18.0	At T-junction turn left to proceed up the hill into Rovarey	Large white house on the left	E	535
41.61	200	19.2	At the bend to the left turn right on a small road		E	539
41.62	600	19.8	Bear right on the track	Downhill	E	544
41.63	700	20.5	At the road junction continue straight ahead		E	529
41.64	600	21.1	At the Stop sign turn left		E	563
41.65	200	21.3	Shortly after passing the church take the steep path to the right		NE	566
41.66	80	21.3	Rejoin the tarmac road bear right then turn to the left towards the Stop sign, then immediately right		E	583

Aosta to Chatillon 30.3 km

Way Point N°	Way Point Distance (metres)	Total Distance (kilometres)	Directions	Verification Point	Compass	Altitude (metres)
41.67	400	21.7	After a steep climb continue straight ahead	Direction Chatillon	E	628
41.68	300	22.0	At the fork bear right on the downhill on the path	Beside two old buildings	E	621
41.69	180	22.2	Cross the bridge and turn right on the tarmac road		SE	628
41.70	200	22.4	In Clapey continue straight ahead	Uphill	E	621
41.71	200	22.6	In Grangeon beside an agriturismo turn right	Through vines	S	625
41.72	200	22.8	After a steep descent take the road to the left	Beside hamlet	E	551
41.73	90	22.9	Join a tarmac road and go straight ahead	Downhill	E	547
41.74	120	23.0	Go straight ahead	Avoid turning to the left	SE	547
41.75	300	23.3	At the T-junction turn left	Direction Chambave	E	498
41.76	800	24.1	At T-junction turn right direction Torino	Enter Chambave	E	485
41.77	300	24.4	Turn left in front of the Café l'Arquebusier	Rue E. Chanoux	E	482
41.78	60	24.5	Turn left on Passage du Barmet. **Note:** for a less strenuous route continue straight ahead along the road on Alternate Route #3		N	484
41.79	70	24.6	Cross the road – rue de Cly - and go straight ahead	Uphill	NE	491
41.80	140	24.7	Return to rue de Cly and continue uphill away from Chambave		E	500
41.81	70	24.8	Turn left on a steeply climbing track and then immediately turn right on a path		N	505

Way Point N°	Way Point Distance (metres)	Total Distance (kilometres)	Directions	Verification Point	Compass	Altitude (metres)
41.82	170	24.9	Arrive beside the waterfall of Rus Chandianaz, turn right around the waterfall	Ignore further turning to the right	E	580
41.83	1700	26.6	At the fork after crossing the mountain-side bear right towards Chatillon	Downhill	S	573
41.84	40	26.7	Cross the tarmac road and go straight ahead down the steep track		E	556
41.85	500	27.2	Go straight ahead	The path passes between a group of houses	E	469
41.86	300	27.5	Before entering the derelict hamlet take the faint path to the left	Skirt the hamlet	E	466
41.87	300	27.8	At T-junction with a tarmac road, turn left on the road		E	473
41.88	180	27.0	At the next bend in the road bear right on the small road		NE	475
41.89	200	28.2	Bear right on the path down the hill towards Chatillon	Beside clearing	E	512
41.90	500	28.7	Continue straight ahead on the tarmac road	Beside fountain	E	489
41.91	500	29,2	On the entry to Chatillon turn right and then immediately left	Via Menabreaz	E	500
41.92	400	29.6	On reaching the Chatillon ring-road take the under-pass and continue straight ahead into the town	Via Menabreaz	E	519
41.93	500	30.1	In the centre of Chatillon turn left . **Note:** caution against the one-way system	Cross the bridge on via Emile Chanoux	E	500
41.94	160	30.2	Turn left	Via Gervasone	NE	495
41.95	40	30.3	Arrive in Chatillon centre in front of the church			505

Alternate #1: this route avoids an unnecessary climb and descent but remains on the roadway (parallel to motorway) throughout

Way Point N°	Way Point Distance (metres)	Total Distance (kilometres)	Directions	Verification Point	Compass	Altitude (metres)
1	0	0	Keep right on the more major road	Località Chef-Lieu	E	586
2	200	0.2	Proceed straight ahead at crossroads		E	585
3	200	0.4	Turn right at crossroads		S	590
4	60	0.5	At crossroads cross over and bear left on Località Angelin parallel to motorway	Murals on little church to left	E	584
5	1200	1.7	Fork left up the hill on Villaggio Olleyes		E	590
6	1800	3.5	At T-junction turn left direction Nus	Villaggio Josuè	E	628
7	1000	45	Rejoin the official route at Way Point #29			683

Useful Contacts

Tourist/Information Offices

Aosta Tourist Office, 8, via Promis - 11100 AOSTA Tel: 0039 (0)16533352
info@aiataosta.com www.aiataosta.com

Internet Cafe

Tetley's Pub, Fraz. 6, La Remise Sarre - 11100 AOSTA

Multimedia Service, 15, corso 26 Febbraio - 11100 AOSTA

Snooker, 6, via Lucat - 11100 AOSTA

Doctor

Veglio Dr. Stefano 46, vl. Pace - 11100 AOSTA Tel: 0039 (0)165 44561

Veterinary

De Luca Dr. Diego, 25, via Brean - 11100 AOSTA Tel: 0039 (0)165 217216

The Alternate Route provides the opportunity to visit Nus, Fenis and Pontey and may be preferred by cyclists as it is entirely on tarmac. The roads are generally quiet except for the area adjacent to the motorway crossing. The route rejoins Alternate Route #3 for the entry into Chatillon.

Way Point N°	Way Point Distance (metres)	Total Distance (kilometres)	Directions	Verification Point	Compass	Altitude (metres)
1	0	0	Keep right in the direction of Nus		SE	559
2	200	0.2	At crossroads at entrance to Nus turn right on via Saint-Barthelemy		S	543
3	170	0.4	Arrive in Nus at junction of via Saint-Barthelemy and via Risorgimento turn left		E	527
4	500	0.9	With the hotel in Nus on the right turn left at the junction with the main road	SS26	E	507
5	160	1.0	Turn right and follow the SR13 over the motorway and river in the direction of Fenis		SE	504
6	2100	3.1	At the crossroads in the centre of Fenis continue straight ahead in the direction of Pontey		E	570
7	3000	6.1	At fork in the road approaching motorway bear right in the direction of Pontey		E	543
8	500	6.6	At fork in the road bear right in the direction of Pontey		E	571
9	4600	11.2	At the crossroads in the centre of Pontey turn left on SR10		NW	532
10	1300	12.5	After crossing motorway turn right to take bridge over river		N	470
11	190	12.7	Rejoin the Alternate Route #3 at the T-junction with the main road and turn right. Alternate Route #3 Way Point #9			457

Alternate Route #3 remains in the lower parts of the valley on minor roads and tracks, only briefly intersecting with the main road. However the route involves a flight of steps. The segment length is very similar to the official route.

Way Point N°	Way Point Distance (metres)	Total Distance (kilometres)	Directions	Verification Point	Compass	Altitude (metres)
1	0	0.0	Continue straight ahead	Rue Emile Chanoux	E	483
2	400	0.4	Turn left at T-junction then take a left fork onto a smaller road, direction Chandianaz	Wooden crucifix on right	E	473
3	300	0.7	Fork left up the hill	Railway on the right	E	473
4	600	1.3	Continue straight ahead direction Chandianaz		E	490
5	150	1.5	Turn right down rough steps	In front of chapel	E	481
6	300	1.8	In Parleaz, bear left of the small station building	Railway on right	E	462
7	400	2.2	Turn right to cross over the railway bridge and then immediately left between the main SS26 and the railway	Bottom of the hill, wooden sign direction Barmaz	E	461
8	200	2.4	Turn left briefly onto the SS26 (pedestrians and riders are probably better staying on the left side because there is a small hard shoulder)		E	456
9	300	2.7	Continue straight ahead. Alternate route rejoins here.		E	456
10	70	2.7	Turn right onto a minor road direction Chatillon	Pèdestre sign	E	457
11	400	3.1	Proceed straight ahead. Ignore Strada Privata sign	River on right	SE	452
12	30	3.2	Turn left through railway tunnel, then turn immediately right to go back onto road		E	451
13	600	3.8	Small road emerges onto SS26, continue along this for about 50 metres and then turn right	Direction Chatillon remain close to railway and river	E	457
14	1500	5.3	At T-junction, left remaining on via Martin Libertà	Large church directly in front	N	500
15	130	5.4	Turn right on via Emile Chanoux into the centre of Chatillon. **Note:** against the flow of traffic - riders dismount	Rejoining Official Route at Way Point #93		501

B&B/Hotel	Price
Hotel Serena 54, via Ponte Romano - 11027 SAINT-VINCENT Tel: 0039 (0)166 512 363	B3
Leon d' Oro 26, via Emilio Chanoux - 11027 SAINT-VINCENT Tel: 0039 (0)166 512 202 leondorosaintvincent@libero.it	B2
Il Tiglio, 18, via Cesare Battisti - 11027 SAINT-VINCENT Tel: 0039 (0)166 5122 crosuno@tin.it www.tigliovacanze.it/	B2
Le Rosier, 1, Frazione Crotache - 11027 SAINT-VINCENT Tel: 0039 (0)166 53 77 26 ada@lerosier.it	B2
Il Torchio, 7, Frazione Capard - 11027 SAINT-VINCENT Tel: 0039 (0)166 512697 info@iltorchio.info www.iltorchio.info	B2
Hotel Bordet 54, via E. Chanoux - 11020 HONE Tel: 0039 (0)125 803 116 delmulino@libero.it	B3
Agriturismo, Le Chemin de la Luge, 17 / 17 A, Fraz. Courtil - 11020 HONE Tel: 0039 (0)125 809 842 chemindeluge@libero.it	B2
Les Souvenirs, 1, Frazione Les Migot - 11020 ISSOGNE Tel: 00 39 339 1009572	B3
Ostello Il Casello, 79, via Stazione - 11029 VERRÈS Tel: 0039 (0)125 921652. www.ilcaselloverres.it	B1
Le Bon Reveil, 85 via Vittorio Emanuele II - 11020 BARD Tel: 0039 (0)125 803986 bonreveil@libero.it	B2
Agriturismo MAISON ROSSET, 0039, via Risorgimento - 11020 NUS Tel: 0039 (0)165 767176 maison.rosset@libero.it www.maisonrosset.it	B3
Agriturismo La GRANGE, Localita Cascine Lys - 11026 PONT SAINT MARTIN Tel: 0039 (0)125 804 253 agriturismolagrange@libero.it	B1
Hotel Grabun, 3, via Nationale per Donnas - 11026 PONT SAINT MARTIN Tel: 0039 (0)125 806069	B2
Al Castel, 8, via Castello, 11026 PONT SAINT MARTIN Tel: 0039 (0)347 4767125	B2

Religious Hostel	Price
Parrocchia San Vincenzo, 7, piazza della Chiesa - 11027 SAINT-VINCENT Tel: 0039 (0)166 512350	Donation
Parrocchia San Giorgio, 1, piazzale San Giorgio - 11020 HONE Tel: 0039 (0)382 815049 Mobile: 0039 338 6178903	Donation

Camping	Price
Paradise Village Camping, 19, via Trieste - 11027 SAINT-VINCENT Tel: 0039 (0)166 513669 info@villageparadise.com www.villageparadise.com	B1

Useful Contacts

Doctor

Greco Dr. Salvatore Ambulatorio Medico, 6, viale Quattro Novembre - 11027 SAINT-VINCENT Tel: 0039 (0)166 512225

Veterinary

Azienda Unita' Sanitaria, 71, via Cretier Amilcare - 11029 VERRES
Tel: 0039 (0)125 921562

Chatillon to Pont Saint Martin 37.6 km

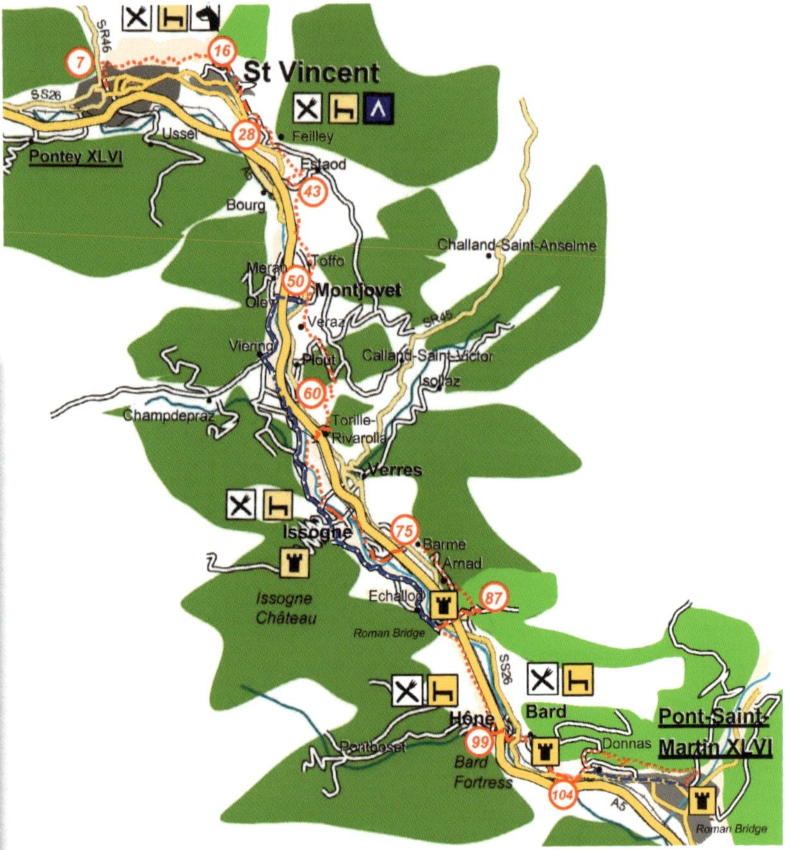

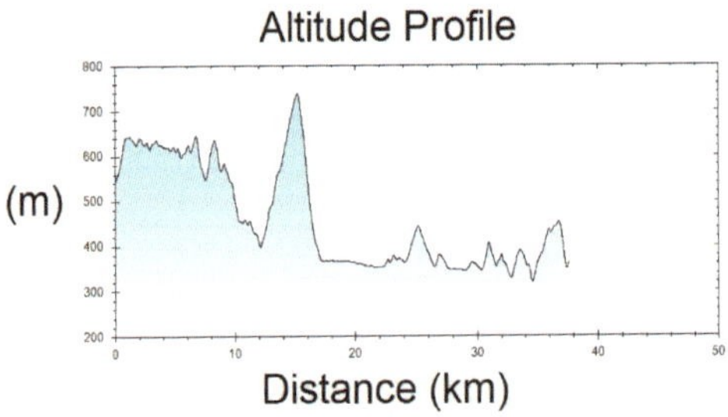

Route Summary: this is a long and tiring section as a result a number of alternatives are offered to reduce distance and eliminate unnecessary climbs. The Official Route follows the hillsides above the valley before crossing and recrossing the river and then returning to hill tracks for the final approach to Pont Saint Martin

Distance from Canterbury: 1115km **Distance to Rome:** 961km

Ascent: 1170m **Descent:** 1344m

Way Point N°	Way Point Distance (metres)	Total Distance (kilometres)	Directions	Verification Point	Compass	Altitude (metres)
42.001	0	0.0	From the front of the church in Chatillon turn left up the hill		NW	624
42.002	50	0.1	Pass beside the church and turn left on the road up the hill	Via Gervasone	N	535
42.003	300	0.3	Take the left fork		N	564
42.004	200	0.6	Cross the small bridge and take the tarmac road up a steep hill to the left		N	588
42.005	100	0.7	Take the road to the left uphill	In Conoz	NW	601
42.006	190	0.8	After a steep climb on the road take the path to the right		NE	627
42.007	50	0.9	Turn right on a tarmac road	The road deteriorates into a track	E	637
42.008	400	1.3	At the fork continue straight ahead		E	652
42.009	500	1.8	Continue straight ahead on the track		E	633
42.010	400	2.2	At the junction with a tarmac road turn right		E	641
42.011	300	2.5	At the stop sign cross straight over and take the path		SE	632
42.012	130	2.6	Continue straight ahead on the tarmac		E	627
42.013	300	2.9	Cross a water-course and continue straight ahead		E	632
42.014	400	3.3	At the crossroads continue straight ahead		E	626
42.015	800	4.1	Continue straight ahead	Ignore the turning to the right	SE	624

Way Point N°	Way Point Distance (metres)	Total Distance (kilometres)	Directions	Verification Point	Compass	Altitude (metres)
42.016	400	4.5	Enter Saint Vincent and continue straight ahead on the tarmac road	Via Monte Bianco	E	618
42.017	200	4.7	Cross the road and turn left uphill		SE	616
42.018	400	5.1	After a short climb turn right on the road		S	624
42.019	70	5.2	At the end of the road take the paved pathway to the left		S	620
42.020	200	5.4	Continue straight ahead	Ignore the turning to the right	E	610
42.021	140	5.5	At the road junction turn right	Downhill	SW	628
42.022	110	5.6	Beside the water-works, turn left towards a yellow house		SE	602
42.023	130	5.8	Bear left onto a steeply descending tarmac road	Via Trois Mosquettaires	SE	599
42.024	600	6.4	Take the right fork downhill and then turn left over a small bridge		SE	627
42.025	120	6.5	Continue straight ahead	Near to the chapel	SW	619
42.026	40	6.5	Take the track to the left	Beside the water-fountain	SW	615
42.027	130	6.7	Descend through the orchards and take a path to the left		S	604
42.028	120	6.8	After a steep climb take the track to the left		E	618
42.029	200	6.0	Bear right on the path	Beside the woods	SE	644
42.030	50	7.0	Turn right on the tarmac road	Frazione Feilley	SE	642
42.031	120	7.2	At the first junction bear right onto a path	Beside the stream	S	635
42.032	160	7.3	Cross a track and continue straight ahead		S	601

Way Point N°	Way Point Distance (metres)	Total Distance (kilometres)	Directions	Verification Point	Compass	Altitude (metres)
42.033	80	7.4	Turn left on the road and continue downhill	Champcillien	SE	584
42.034	200	7.6	In front of the house take the track to the right	Champ de Vigne	SE	576
42.035	200	7.8	At the stone house turn to the left	Through the orchards	SE	546
42.036	170	7.0	Near to the house continue on the track		SE	556
42.037	120	8.1	After a steep climb in the woods turn left in the clearing		SE	578
42.038	60	8.1	After a short climb bear left on the track across the hillside		SE	589
42.039	150	8.3	Bear right on the cart track		SE	618
42.040	200	8.5	Continue straight ahead on the tarmac	Chenal	E	633
42.041	70	8.6	Take the first turning to the right and immediately right again	Downhill	SW	640
42.042	500	9.1	Beside the clearing bear left on the cart track		SE	567
42.043	300	9.4	Cross the tarmac road and continue straight ahead along the roadway	Ignore the turnings to the left	S	588
42.044	500	9.9	Bear left on the road, downhill	Beside Castello di Montjovet	S	550
42.045	1000	10.9	Ignore the turning to the right and continue straight ahead on the track	Balmas	SE	452
42.046	140	11.0	Continue straight ahead	Ignore the small road to the right	S	447
42.047	900	11.9	Continue straight ahead on the tarmac	Toffo	SE	436

Chatillon to Pont Saint Martin 37.6 km

Way Point N°	Way Point Distance (metres)	Total Distance (kilometres)	Directions	Verification Point	Compass	Altitude (metres)
42.048	300	12.2	At the junction turn right on the track		S	427
42.049	150	12.3	Beside a group of houses turn right		SW	408
42.050	80	12.4	Arrive in Montjovet and take the road to the left up the hill		SW	401
42.051	90	12.5	At the first bend to the left take the path to the right	Downhill	S	394
42.052	150	12.7	Turn left, then immediately right. **Note:** there is a climb of 400m ahead on the official route. To avoid the climb turn right and follow Alternate Route #1 across the valley	Near the church	S	410
42.053	600	13.3	Join a tarmac road and bear left	Uphill	S	485
42.054	600	13.9	Bear left onto a path	Steeply uphill	E	530
42.055	150	14.0	Continue straight ahead on the road and after 50m take a small path to the right		SE	556
42.056	700	14.7	Turn left on the path between the houses	Cuignonaz	SE	600
42.057	100	14.8	Rejoin the road and bear left	Uphill	S	618
42.058	800	15.6	After a long steep climb take the track to the right		SW	719
42.059	300	15.9	Arrive at top of the hill and continue straight on the path	Downhill	S	744
42.060	300	16.2	Continue straight ahead downhill	Beside isolated house	S	689
42.061	1100	17.3	Continue on the road through the village	Torille	W	396
42.062	200	17.5	At the T-junction with the SS26 turn left and then right under the motorway		SW	374

Way Point N°	Way Point Distance (metres)	Total Distance (kilometres)	Directions	Verification Point	Compass	Altitude (metres)
42.063	200	17.7	Continue straight ahead	Ignore the turning to the left beside the pylon	W	365
42.064	110	17.8	At the T-junction turn left	The river is immediately to the right	S	366
42.065	800	18.6	Cross a small bridge and bear right	Remaining on the bank of the river	S	364
42.066	700	19.3	At the T-junction turn right	Over the river bridge	SW	365
42.067	160	19.5	Immediately after crossing the river turn left. **Note:** the route can be reduced by 2.6km by taking the next turning to the right on Alternate Route #2	Frazione Fleuran	SE	366
42.068	1100	20.6	At the T-junction turn left	Recross the river Dora	NE	360
42.069	180	20.8	After crossing the bridge immediately turn right	Keeping river close on the right	SE	361
42.070	400	21.2	Take the right fork downhill and then turn left over a small bridge	Towards the river	SE	357
42.071	700	21.9	Continue straight ahead	Beside the river	E	352
42.072	120	21.0	Turn left	Towards the motorway	NE	352
42.073	190	22.2	Turn right on the tarmac road	Bridge over the motorway	NE	352
42.074	600	22.8	At the T-junction turn right and immediately left	SS26	NE	354
42.075	200	22.0	Take the road to the right		SE	372
42.076	300	23.3	At the T-junction turn left		SE	359
42.077	400	23.7	Enter Barme and continue straight ahead	Ignore the turning on the right	S	373

Chatillon to Pont Saint Martin 37.6 km

Way Point N°	Way Point Distance (metres)	Total Distance (kilometres)	Directions	Verification Point	Compass	Altitude (metres)
42.078	200	23.9	At the Stop sign turn left	Frazione Sisan	SE	365
42.079	500	24.4	Just after the restaurant Buon Convento take the road to the right		SW	371
42.080	130	24.5	At the T-junction turn left	Parrocchiale di San Martino	E	360
42.081	130	24.6	Turn left and slightly uphill		E	364
42.082	300	24.9	At the first junction bear left	Into Prouve	SE	385
42.083	200	25.1	After a short , steep climb continue straight ahead		SE	408
42.084	130	25.3	Beside a water-fountain turn left		NE	413
42.085	60	25.3	Take the path to the right		SE	426
42.086	200	25.5	Continue straight ahead	Beside Castello Valaise	SE	437
42.087	200	25.7	At T-junction turn right	Strada Regionale di Arnad	W	443
42.088	200	25.9	Take the first turning to the left		S	418
42.089	90	26.0	After crossing the bridge immediately turn right		W	420
42.090	300	26.3	Turn left and then right	Towards the sports ground	SW	392
42.091	300	26.6	Follow the track under the motorway		SW	377
42.092	130	26.8	Take the right fork and cross straight over the main road		W	366
42.093	200	26.9	Continue straight ahead	Ignore a turning to the left	SW	355
42.094	80	27.0	Continue straight ahead	Towards Ponte di Echallod	W	352
42.095	150	27.2	Cross the bridge and turn left. **Note:** alternate Route #2 joins from the right	Beside the river	SE	357

Way Point N°	Way Point Distance (metres)	Total Distance (kilometres)	Directions	Verification Point	Compass	Altitude (metres)
42.096	1000	28.2	Turn right onto track just before Autostrada bridge	VF sign	SE	347
42.097	1500	29.7	Proceed straight ahead into Hône		S	345
42.098	400	30.1	Cross the road and continue straight ahead		S	364
42.099	400	30.5	At crossroads turn left to go under Autostrada bridge	Between château and river	E	354
42.100	150	30.6	At fork bear right to cross over the river bridge		E	350
42.101	400	31.0	After bridge turn right on SS26 and then bear left on the narrow road into the old town. **Note:** there has been considerable road and building work blocking the latter parts of the road. The main road offers an alternative to Way Point #103 but it is very busy and difficult for all groups	Fortress on the right	S	357
42.102	500	31.5	Continue straight ahead downhill	Ignore the turning towards the fortress	SE	414
42.103	1000	32.5	Turn left beside the SS26 and take the pavement on the left		E	386
42.104	500	33.0	Bear away from the main road towards the centre of Donnas	Pass the Arch of Donnas	E	343
42.105	300	33.3	Turn left up the hill. **Note:** to avoid further climbing and to reduce the route by 2.3km follow viale Selve and Alternate Route #3	Via Jean Bréan	N	326
42.106	400	33.7	After a steep climb turn right	Towards Rovarey	E	381

Chatillon to Pont Saint Martin 37.6 km

Way Point N°	Way Point Distance (metres)	Total Distance (kilometres)	Directions	Verification Point	Compass	Altitude (metres)
42.107	200	33.9	Turn right towards Rovarey		SE	393
42.108	400	34.3	Turn left	Rue Barme	SE	350
42.109	400	34.7	Turn left	Via Rondevacca	E	320
42.110	150	34.9	Turn left on the steeply climbing road		E	319
42.111	600	35.5	Take the left fork		E	382
42.112	400	35.9	Take the right fork		E	429
42.113	1100	36.0	Take the steep track to the right	Track marked number 1	S	450
42.114	120	37.1	Go straight ahead on the tarmac		SW	420
42.115	160	37.3	Cross the road and continue straight ahead on the track		W	386
42.116	60	37.3	Bear left downhill	Via Perloz	SW	366
42.117	120	37.4	At the T-junction turn left. **Note:** alternate Route #3 joins from the right	Via Emile Lanoux	SE	346
42.118	200	37.6	Arrive in Pont Saint Martin beside the church			360

The Alternate Route, slightly shorter, quickly crosses the river Dora and the motorway and proceeds along tracks and small roads on the valley floor

Way Point N°	Way Point Distance (metres)	Total Distance (kilometres)	Directions	Verification Point	Compass	Altitude (metres)
1	0	0.0	By the church in Monjovet take the tarmac road to the right		W	452
2	60	0.1	Bear left	After passing a flight of steps on the right	SW	395
3	70	0.1	Cross the SS62 and take the road over the river and under the motorway	Direction Oley	W	391
4	500	0.6	Follow the road as it turns left and parallel to the motorway	VF sign, Frazione Oley	S	379
5	1700	2.3	At T-junction in Viering turn left down the hill	Turn in the middle of a group of houses	SE	384
6	400	2.7	Turn right onto a gravel track directly in front of a tunnel going under the railway. **Note:** cyclists can remain on the road, pass under the Autostrada on via Giordano Freydoz until turning back under the Autostrada at the junction with the SR6, rejoining at Way Point #9	Keep railway close on left	S	375
7	300	3.0	Track leads into open field, cross straight over and then bear left to join an unmade road, which emerges onto a tarmac road	Railway directly on left	SE	378
8	400	3.4	Turn left at the T-junction on SR6	Keep railway to the left	SE	375
9	200	3.6	Turn right directly in front of a tunnel passing under the Autostrada	Large concrete wall on right. Towards the right bank of the river	S	374
10	1400	5.0	Turn left at the T-junction to follow the river	Keep railway to the left	SE	369
11	1400	6.4	Arrive in Fleuran with river bridge on the left at Way Point #67 on the main route	Large electricity pylons and river on left		366

Alternate Route #2 from Fleuran to Echallod 4.5km

The Alternate Route, reduces total distance by 2.6km and proceeds on minor roads and tracks remaining on the right side of the river and passing through the pleasant town of Issogne

Way Point N°	Way Point Distance (metres)	Total Distance (kilometres)	Directions	Verification Point	Compass	Altitude (metres)
1	0	0.0	Turn right into a narrow alleyway, direction Issogne on a cycle path	Large electricity pylons and river on left	SW	367
2	130	0.1	Turn left at junction at the top of the rise		SE	377
3	800	0.9	Turn right direction Issogne Château and church		SW	381
4	110	1.0	Turn left into a narrow street passing the Cafeteria Paninoteca	Château on right	S	391
5	50	1.1	Turn left onto Frazione Pied-de-Ville		SE	390
6	400	1.5	Turn left and immediately right onto cycle route, direction Arnad	Parallel to river	SE	364
7	1300	2.8	Proceed on the road	Closer to river	SE	356
8	900	3.7	At crossroads turn left parallel to river		S	357
9	300	4.0	Turn right direction Hône	River on left	SE	354
10	500	4.5	Rejoin Official Route at Way Point #95	River bridge on the left		358

Alternate Route #3 from Donnas to Pont Saint Martin 2.5km

The Alternate Route, reduces total distance by 2.3km but quickly returns to the busy SS62, following this and the via Nazionale through the centre of Pont Saint Martin

Way Point N°	Way Point Distance (metres)	Total Distance (kilometres)	Directions	Verification Point	Compass	Altitude (metres)
1	0	0.0	Continue straight ahead on via Selve		E	326
2	300	0.3	At the T-junction with the SS62 turn left		E	327
3	1600	1.9	At the roundabout take the last exit direction Pont Saint Martin		E	327
4	600	2.5	Rejoin the Official Route at Way Point #117			345

Useful Contacts

Tourist/Information Offices

Agenzia Turistica Locale, 1, corso Vercelli - 10015 IVREA Tel: 0039 (0)125618131
http://www.turismotorino.org/index.php?id=512&navCmd=reset

Doctor

Brescia Dr. Graziella, 4, via Delle Miniere - 10015 IVREA Tel: 0039 (0)125 45432

Veterinary

Ghirardo Dr. Michele, 5, piazza Freguglia C. - 10015 IVREA Tel: 0039 (0)125 425065

Hotel/B&B	Price
Hotel la Gria, via Aosta 240 - 10013 BORGOFRANCO D'IVREA Tel: 0039 (0)125751009	B2
I Tre Ciliegi, 24, via Mulini - Fraz. Biò - 10010 BORGOFRANCO D'IVREA Tel: 0039 (0)125 752216 v.baruzzi@flashnet.it	B2
La Rampichina, 24, via Ghirardo - Fraz. Baio Dora - 10010 BORGOFRANCO D'IVREA Tel: 0039 (0)125 750101 demetra53@libero.it	B2
L' Ospitalita del Castello, 7, piazza Conte Rinaldo - 10015 IVREA Mobile: 0039 348 4527017 info@lospitalitadelcastello.it	B2
Casa dei Gelsomini, 16, Canton Torfano - 10015 IVREA Mobile: 0039 347 72373734	B2

Religious Hostel	Price
L' Ospitalita de il Castello, 7, piazza Conte Rinaldo - 10010 SETTIMO VITTONE Tel: 0039 (0)125 659083 info@lospitalitadelcastello.it	B1
Salesiano Seminary, 58, via S. Giovanni Bosco - 10015 IVREA Tel: 0039 (0)125 420500	B2
Ostello Canoa Club, 1d, via Dora Baltea - 10015 IVREA Tel: 0039 (0)125 40186	Donation
Eporeidese, 58, via San Giovanni Bosco - 10015 IVREA Tel: 0039 (0)125 627268	B2

Camping	Price
Lago san Michele, via Lago san Michele - 10015 IVREA Tel: 0039 (0)125 616195	B1

Lillianes
SR44
Donnas
Pont-Saint-Martin XLVI
Roman Bridge
Autostrada Aosta-Torino A5
10
Carema
Valle d'Aosta
Piemonte
27
Torre-Danielle
Quincinetto
Cesnola
Settimo Vittore
46
Tavanasco
12
Montestrutto
Nomaglio
Quassolo
59
Borgofranco d'Ivrea
Baio Dora
73
Calea
Montalto Dora
SS26
Dora Baltea
Ivrea XLV
20
89
Duomo de Santa Maria
SS228
A5
Florano Canavese
22
Torre di Santo Stefano
Banchette
SS565

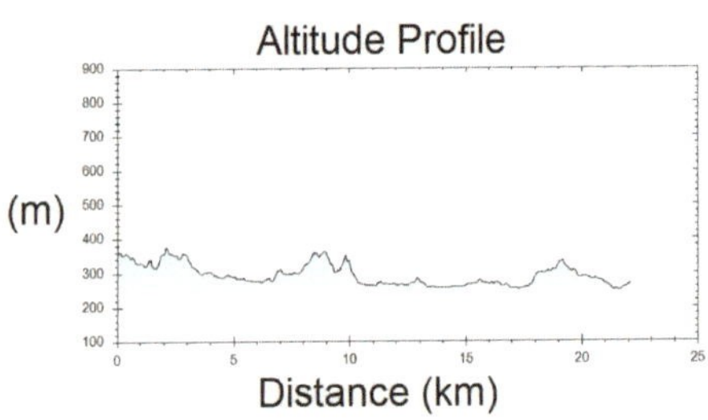
Altitude Profile
(m)
900
800
700
600
500
400
300
200
100
0
5
10
15
20
25
Distance (km)

Route Summary: this shorter section continues on pathways and tracks along the hillsides and through the old vineyards to the east of the river Dora. Extra caution is necessary where the route intersects with with the busy SS62 on a number of occasions.

Distance from Canterbury: 1153km **Distance from Canterbury:** 923km

Ascent: 555m **Descent:** 637m

Way Point N°	Way Point Distance (metres)	Total Distance (kilometres)	Directions	Verification Point	Compass	Altitude (metres)
43.001	0	0.0	From the piazza primo Maggio go straight ahead on the main road	Via Emile Chanoux	SE	350
43.002	200	0.2	Cross the river bridge	Roman bridge to the left	SE	351
43.003	100	0.3	Bear left on the small road	Via Boschetto	S	355
43.004	200	0.5	Continue straight ahead	End of the tarmac	S	353
43.005	400	0.9	At the junction with the main road turn left on the smaller road	Rue Sant'Erasmo	SE	328
43.006	500	1.4	Turn left on the small tarmac road		E	320
43.007	70	1.5	Take the passage ahead between two fences and near to a condominium		SE	328
43.008	100	1.6	Bear left on the tarmac road		S	334
43.009	200	1.8	At the sharp bend to the left bear right on the steep path downhill	Towards the houses	S	314
43.010	90	1.9	Beside a house take the pathway to the left between the vines. **Note:** turn right and take Alternate Route #1 to bypass the old town of Carema		E	313
43.011	120	1.0	At the first turning, turn right up the hill	Signed: Sentiero dei Vigneti	SE	338
43.012	160	2.1	Continue straight ahead in the direction of Carema	Beside la Cappella di San Rocco	E	356
43.013	500	2.6	Continue straight ahead in the pedestrian zone of Carema		SE	352
43.014	300	2.9	At the end of via Roma turn left	Via Basiglia	E	343

Pont Saint Martin to Ivrea 22.1 km

Way Point N°	Way Point Distance (metres)	Total Distance (kilometres)	Directions	Verification Point	Compass	Altitude (metres)
43.015	60	3.0	Turn right	In front of the church	S	353
43.016	140	3.1	At the bottom of the road turn left and immediately right	In front of a medieval house	S	355
43.017	50	3.2	Cross the tarmac road and continue straight ahead		W	350
43.018	90	3.3	Cross another tarmac road and continue straight ahead before turning left		SW	335
43.019	110	3.4	Take the left fork and follow the track	Between the vines	S	319
43.020	120	3.5	Take the right fork on the paved road		SW	316
43.021	110	3.6	Take the left fork on the track		S	307
43.022	130	3.8	At the junction with the main road turn left. **Note:** caution for traffic. The Alternate Route joins from the right	SS26	SE	297
43.023	100	3.9	Continue straight ahead	It is possible to gain some protection from the traffic by crossing behind the crash barrier	S	297
43.024	150	4.0	Continue on the main road	SS26	S	302
43.025	800	4.8	Turn left. **Note:** cyclists may wish to avoid further climbing by going straight ahead on Alternate Route #2	Direction Airale	SE	287
43.026	200	5.0	Continue straight ahead on via Giasso	Beside small church	SE	292
43.027	300	5.3	Continue straight ahead on the track		SE	284
43.028	180	5.5	Cross the small bridge and continue straight ahead		E	283
43.029	80	5.6	Bear right on a tarmac road		S	285

Way Point N°	Way Point Distance (metres)	Total Distance (kilometres)	Directions	Verification Point	Compass	Altitude (metres)
43.030	200	5.8	Turn left towards the churchyard	Pass through Torredaniele	E	277
43.031	90	5.8	Turn right at the edge of the commune		SE	278
43.032	120	5.0	At the T-junction turn right		S	275
43.033	80	6.0	Before reaching the main road turn left on the dirt track	Parallel to SS26	SE	276
43.034	800	6.8	Bear left on a track between the vines		SE	279
43.035	300	7.2	Continue straight ahead	Enter the village of Cesnola	S	307
43.036	80	7.2	Bear right on a tarmac road down the hill	Beside water trough	SW	311
43.037	100	7.3	Take the first turning to the left into the countryside	The way quickly becomes a track	S	297
43.038	700	8.0	Continue straight ahead	The track becomes a tarmac road	S	300
43.039	90	8.1	Turn left uphill	Beside the ruined church in Settimo Vittonea	SE	304
43.040	150	8.3	Continue uphill on the tarmac road		SE	321
43.041	60	8.3	Continue straight ahead on the pavement		E	323
43.042	200	8.5	At the end of the pavement continue straight ahead		E	336
43.043	70	8.6	Turn left on the paved road		E	344
43.044	80	8.7	Turn right	In front of the church	SE	358
43.045	70	8.8	Turn left on the dirt road on the other side of the gates with the red and white sign	Beside the San Lorenzo complex	E	354
43.046	80	8.8	Bear left on the path		SE	356
43.047	190	9.0	Bear left uphill on the tarmac		S	353

Pont Saint Martin to Ivrea 22.1 km

Way Point N°	Way Point Distance (metres)	Total Distance (kilometres)	Directions	Verification Point	Compass	Altitude (metres)
43.048	200	9.2	Continue straight ahead on the path through the vines		S	357
43.049	400	9.6	Take the pathway to the left	Near a small tarmac road	S	304
43.050	200	9.8	Continue straight ahead	Cross tunnel	S	307
43.051	50	9.9	Bear left on the steep tarmac road	Uphill	SE	307
43.052	160	10.0	Continue straight ahead on the track	Beside the hamlet of Casellino	SE	332
43.053	100	10.1	At the first turning on the track turn right downhill	View of Castello Montestrutto	S	350
43.054	150	10.3	Bear right towards Montestrutto		W	321
43.055	300	10.6	Turn left on the via Principale	In the centre of Montestrutto	SE	274
43.056	300	10.9	Take the track to the left around the house	Beside electricity pylon	SE	264
43.057	180	11.1	Continue straight ahead on the track		SE	263
43.058	180	11.2	Take the tarmac road to the left		SE	262
43.059	1500	12.7	Turn left	Beside the church of San Germano	E	263
43.060	300	13.0	Turn right	Via del Buonumore	S	274
43.061	500	13.5	Turn left on the track	Into the countryside	S	257
43.062	500	14.0	Return to the tarmac and continue straight ahead	In view of Borgofranco d'Ivrea	S	256
43.063	200	14.2	At the Stop sign cross over the road and turn right		W	255
43.064	120	14.4	Turn left	Via Cavour	S	256
43.065	300	14.7	In piazza Ruffini, in Borgofranco, turn left on via delle Chiese	Beneath Torre Porta	E	258

Way Point N°	Way Point Distance (metres)	Total Distance (kilometres)	Directions	Verification Point	Compass	Altitude (metres)
43.066	110	14.8	Turn left in piazza del Ricetto and then right on the paved road	Via Andrate	E	259
43.067	200	14.0	Continue straight ahead on the tarmac road		E	258
43.068	170	15.1	Bear right	Via Mulini	SE	261
43.069	120	15.3	Bear right on the track		S	265
43.070	200	15.5	At the first junction in the woods bear right		S	267
43.071	200	15.7	Take the track to the right		S	274
43.072	800	16.5	Continue straight ahead	Ignore the turning to the right	S	270
43.073	500	16.0	Continue straight ahead on the tarmac road	Near an old quarry	S	255
43.074	300	17.3	At the first junction turn left	Via Aldo Balla	S	252
43.075	200	17.5	In the piazza in Montalto turn left	Via Casana	E	254
43.076	120	17.6	Turn right	Via Cappella	S	259
43.077	90	17.7	At the T-junction turn left and then right		SE	255
43.078	120	17.8	Continue straight ahead up the hill	Via Matteotti	E	260
43.079	400	18.2	At the crossroads go straight ahead on the larger road	The road quickly makes a double bend	SE	295
43.080	300	18.5	Turn right	Beside the chapel	SW	297
43.081	160	18.6	Continue straight ahead on the track		SW	304
43.082	300	18.9	Turn left on a track	Direction Cappella di San Pietro	SE	307
43.083	300	19.3	At the top of the hill continue straight ahead on the track		SE	334

Pont Saint Martin to Ivrea 22.1 km

Way Point N°	Way Point Distance (metres)	Total Distance (kilometres)	Directions	Verification Point	Compass	Altitude (metres)
43.084	300	19.6	Continue straight ahead on the tarmac road	Beside Cappella di San Pietro	S	313
43.085	150	19.7	At the road junction take the track to the left		E	303
43.086	200	19.9	Continue straight ahead on the tarmac road		E	290
43.087	80	19.0	Continue straight ahead on the tarmac road		SE	286
43.088	200	20.2	Turn right	Via Sant'Ulderico	SW	288
43.089	300	20.5	Continue straight ahead on the dirt road		S	280
43.090	300	20.8	At the bottom continue on the tarmac		SW	278
43.091	300	21.1	Continue straight ahead on the pavement		S	268
43.092	500	21.6	Turn left	Beside supermarket car park	E	248
43.093	110	21.7	Turn right at the edge of the commune	Beside the old city walls of Ivrea	SW	249
43.094	120	21.8	Continue straight ahead across the road		SW	257
43.095	140	21.9	Turn left	Via Amedeo di Castellamonte	S	257
43.096	60	22.0	Turn left	Under the arch	SE	261
43.097	60	22.1	Bear left uphill towards the Castle	Via Torri	SE	266
43.098	60	22.1	Arrive in the centre of Ivrea	Beside the Duomo		266

Alternate Route #1 bypassing Carema 1.2km
The Alternate Route bypasses the the old centre of Carema saving 600m

Way Point N°	Way Point Distance (metres)	Total Distance (kilometres)	Directions	Verification Point	Compass	Altitude (metres)
1	0	0.0	At the T-junction turn right towards the main road and proceed on the footpath to the left		SE	313
2	90	0.1	Continue straight ahead on the small paved road		S	320
3	70	0.2	Bear left on the tarmac road	Via Provinciale	SE	314
4	600	0.8	At the junction with the main roads continue straight ahead on the pavement	SS26	S	300
5	170	0.9	Bear left away from the main road	Via Vittorio Emanuele	S	298
6	170	1.1	Continue straight ahead on the main road keeping to the left side. **Note:** pay close attention to the traffic	SS26	SE	299
7	80	1.2	Rejoin the official route at Way Point #22 and continue straight ahead on the main road	SS26		297

Alternate route #2 from Airale to Ivrea 17.0km
The Alternate Route, a similar distance to the official route, is less strenuous and better suited to cyclists. It follows quiet roads and tracks on the western side of the river before taking busier roads on the final entry to Ivrea

Way Point N°	Way Point Distance (metres)	Total Distance (kilometres)	Directions	Verification Point	Compass	Altitude (metres)
1	0	0.0	Continue straight ahead on the main road	SS26	S	286
2	600	0.6	Turn right over the bridge direction Quincinetto	Cross Dora Baltea	SW	280
3	500	1.1	Bear right with petrol station on right	Motorway toll station on left	S	286
4	150	1.3	Bear left direction Campo Sportivo	Via 4 Novembre	SE	286
5	400	1.6	At fork bear left to cross over the Autostrada		NE	283
6	120	1.8	Having crossed over the Autostrada and come down the ramp turn sharp right onto a track	Track runs between the railway and Autostrada	SE	280

Alternates Routes

CONTINUED						
Way Point N°	Way Point Distance (metres)	Total Distance (kilometres)	Directions	Verification Point	Compass	Altitude (metres)
7	600	2.4	Bear right to ford the stream		SE	280
8	80	2.5	Turn right to proceed alongside the motorway on your right		S	278
9	170	2.6	At T-junction with road turn left and continue beside the Autostrada		SE	279
10	900	3.5	At crossroads turn right under the Autostrada to enter Tavagnasco	River bridge to the left at junction	SW	274
11	120	3.6	At crossroads turn left to follow via Roma		S	280
12	400	4.0	Turn left beside large church to recross Autostrada		E	271
13	300	4.3	At T-junction turn right	Follow road between railway and Autostrada	S	267
14	2400	6.7	At crossroads with river bridge to the left turn right direction Quassolo	Go under road bridge	W	256
15	160	6.9	At crossroads turn left on via Garibaldi		SW	264
16	200	7.1	Bear left onto the via San Gregorio		S	262
17	400	7.5	Turn left to cross over a small bridge and then turn immediately right - via San Rocco	Keep Autostrada on your left	S	256
18	1300	8.8	In Baio Dora bear left on via Commendatore Pietro Presbitero	Direction Banchette	S	258
19	190	8.0	Road bears right and left	Via Presbitero	S	256
20	3100	12.1	At T-junction turn left direction Ivrea	SP69	SE	247
21	2300	14.4	At the second roundabout take the last exit via Roma		E	243

CONTINUED

Way Point N°	Way Point Distance (metres)	Total Distance (kilometres)	Directions	Verification Point	Compass	Altitude (metres)
22	600	14.0	At fork bear left into the village on via Roma		SE	245
23	500	15.5	At T-junction turn left to proceed into Ivrea	Via delle Miniere	E	252
24	300	15.8	At T-junction turn left towards Ivrea centre	Via delle Miniere	NE	262
25	800	16.6	At T-junction turn left towards Ivrea centre	Corso Constantino Nigra	N	247
26	200	16.8	At T-junction turn right after crossing the bridge over Dora Baltea	River on right after turn	NE	246
27	50	16.8	Turn left on the via Riva	Away from the river	N	248
28	110	16.9	At the T-junction turn right	Via Arduino	E	262
29	180	17.1	Take the second turning on the left		NW	260
30	70	17.2	Turn sharp right and then immediately left up the steps	Via delle Torri	NW	265
31	40	17.2	Arrive at the end of the section in the centre of Ivrea	Beside the Duomo		266

Alternates Routes

Ivrea is on the road leading out of the Aosta Valley and lies in a basin that, in prehistoric times, formed a great lake. Today a number of smaller lakes dot the area around the town. During the 20th century its primary claim to fame was as the base of operations for Olivetti, a once well-known manufacturer of typewriters, mechanical calculators and, later, computers. When Olivetti closed its operations the population dropped to 30% of its former level.
The town first appears in history as a Roman cavalry station founded in 100 BC and set to guard one of the traditional invasion routes into northern Italy over the Alps. The Latin name of the town, Eporedia (meaning: "place to change horses"), has long since vanished into the mists of time, but still appears as the root of the name of the town residents, who are known as "eporediesi" in Italian and as "Eporedians" in English.
After the fall of the Western Roman Empire, Ivrea became the seat of a duchy under the Lombards (6th-8th centuries). Later Ivrea was disputed between the bishops, the marquis of Monferrato and the House of Savoy. In 1356 Ivrea was acquired by Amadeus VI of Savoy. With the exception of the brief French conquest at the end of the 16th century, Ivrea remained under Savoy until 1800. On May 26 of that year Napoleon Bonaparte entered the city along with his victorious troops and left in 1814 after his fall.
Main sights:
The Cathedral, probably erected in the 4th century AD over a Pagan temple. The current neo-classical façade is from the 19th century. The main art piece of the interior is the Miraculous Resurrection of a Child (second half of 15th century), attributed to Nicolas Robert. The sacristy has two panes by Defendente Ferrari. The cathedral is also seat of the tomb of Blessed Thaddeus McCarthy.

The Capitular Library, not far from the Cathedral, houses an important collection of codices from 7th-15th centuries.
The small Gothic church of San Bernardino, which houses a notable cycle portraying the Life and Passion of Christ by Giovanni Martino Spanzotti (1480-1490).
The Museum Pier Alessandro Garda has some interesting archaeological findings and a collection of Japanese art pieces. It is located on the large piazza Ottinetti.
The Open Air Museum of Modern Architecture, inaugurated in 2001 - a show of the main edifices (some by leading architects of the time) built by Olivetti from the 1950s onwards. The remains of a Roman theatre from the first century west of the city centre.
The Ponte Vecchio, dating back to 100 AD. Originally built in wood and rebuilt in stone in 1716.
The St. Stephen Tower dating back to 11th century. A romanesque bell tower built in 1041 for the Benedictine order, located between Hotel La Serra and Dora Baltea.

Today, Ivrea is best known for its Battle of the Oranges, involving thousands of townspeople, divided into nine combat teams, who throw oranges at each other - with considerable violence - during the traditional carnival days, Sunday, Monday and Tuesday. Unfortunately (or fortunately, depending on your view), the carnival takes place in February and ends with a solemn funeral on the night of Fat Tuesday.

Hotel/B&B	Price
Casa Francigena, via al Castello - 13883 ROPPOLO Tel: 0039 (0)39 20 55 546	Donation
Agriturismo, Barale Cascina Cason Vecchio Str. Lista - 13048 SANTHIA Tel: 0039 (0)161 939897	B2
Albergo s. Massimo, corso Xxv Aprile 18 - 13048 SANTHIA Tel: 0039 (0)161 94617 sanmassimo.ss143@tele2.it	B2
Hotel Piccadilly, 51, via XXV Aprile - 13048 SANTHIA Tel: 0039 (0)161 921196	B2

Camping	Price
Camping Internazionale del Sole, 45, Località Comuna - 13886 VIVERONE Tel: 0039 (0)161 98169	B1
Camping la Rocca, 35, viale Lungo Lago - 13886 VIVERONE Tel: 0039 (0)161 98416	B1

Ivrea Cathedral

Useful Contacts

Doctor

Bossola Dr. Carlo Medico Chirurgo, 20, via Raffaello Sanzio - 13048 SANTHIA
Tel: 0039 (0)161 921201

Veterinary

Basso Dr. Laura, 64, via Antonio Gramsci - 13048 SANTHIA
Tel: 0039 (0)161 921166

Ivrea to Santhià 37.9 km

Route Summary: a long section largely undertaken on the final wooded slopes of the Piedmont. There is an opportunity to break the journey in the area near Lake Viverone

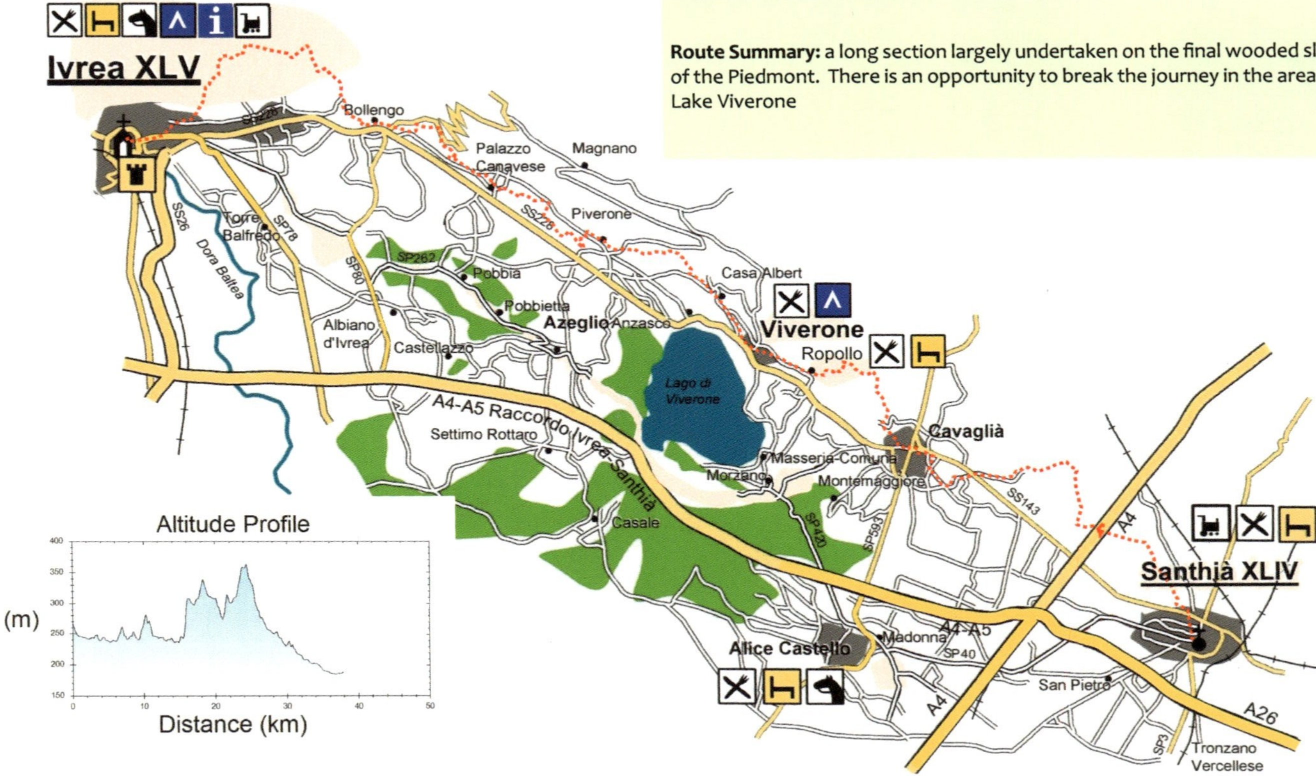

Distance from Canterbury: 1175km | **Distance to Rome:** 901km

Ascent: 351m | **Descent:** 432m

Way Point N°	Way Point Distance (metres)	Total Distance (kilometres)	Directions	Verification Point	Compass	Altitude (metres)
44.001	0	0.0	From the piazza del Duomo in Ivrea, take the path downhill towards the city centre. **Note:** horse-riders should start at the next Way Point at the foot of the steps on via Vaglia		SE	266
44.002	60	0.1	At bottom of the steps turn left		E	264
44.003	200	0.3	Turn left	Via Palestro	E	259
44.004	300	0.6	In piazza Balla go straight ahead	Via d'Azeglio	E	250
44.005	400	0.0	Bear left	Via Cascinette	NE	246
44.006	300	1.3	Continue straight ahead		E	245
44.007	400	1.7	At the roundabout bear left	Via Cascinette	NE	244
44.008	400	2.1	Take the left fork	Via Monte della Guardia	N	242
44.009	400	2.5	At the T-junction turn right		NE	244
44.010	120	2.6	Take the small road to the left into the country		NE	242
44.011	300	2.9	Turn left		N	244
44.012	200	3.1	Continue straight ahead on the path	Keep Lago Campagna on the left	NE	246
44.013	400	3.5	At the end of the path keep straight ahead across the parking area		SE	246
44.014	110	3.6	Take the tarmac road to the left		NE	240
44.015	200	3.8	At the T-junction turn left and immediately right	Via Gorrere	E	239
44.016	110	3.9	At the first junction turn left on the track into the woods		N	239
44.017	200	4.1	At the next junction turn right		E	243
44.018	1300	5.4	On leaving the woods take the track to the left	Beside large field	NE	237

Ivrea to Santhià 37.9 km

Way Point N°	Way Point Distance (metres)	Total Distance (kilometres)	Directions	Verification Point	Compass	Altitude (metres)
44.019	400	5.8	At the Stop sign turn right on the tarmac		S	240
44.020	600	6.4	At the main road, cross over, turn left and continue on the right-hand side of the road		E	241
44.021	200	6.6	Turn right	Via Vivier	SE	250
44.022	180	6.8	At the fork keep left	Remain on via Vivier	SE	253
44.023	200	6.0	Continue downhill on the main road		S	262
44.024	300	7.3	Take the tarmac road on the left	Towards the cemetery	S	248
44.025	300	7.6	Turn left	Via Bollengo	SE	241
44.026	700	8.3	In Bollengo turn right	Before the chapel of San Rocco	SW	248
44.027	80	8.4	Cross the road and turn left		E	244
44.028	300	8.7	In the centre of Bollengo turn right	Direction Biella	E	253
44.029	180	8.8	Continue straight ahead	Parco Giochi	E	248
44.030	110	8.9	Continue straight ahead		E	245
44.031	140	9.1	Cross the main road and continue straight ahead		E	243
44.032	500	9.6	At the bend to the right turn left on the small path	Towards the church of San Pietro	N	247
44.033	160	9.8	At the church turn right on the tarmac road		SE	256
44.034	1600	11.3	At the bottom of the hill turn left on the main road	Direction Piverone	SE	245
44.035	900	12.3	In the palazzo Canavese turn right	Via Garibaldi	SE	245
44.036	300	12.6	In piazza Olivetti turn left on via dei Mulini and immediately right	Via 20 Settembre	SE	243
44.037	140	12.7	Take the next turning to the left		SE	245

Way Point N°	Way Point Distance (metres)	Total Distance (kilometres)	Directions	Verification Point	Compass	Altitude (metres)
44.038	110	12.8	Turn left	Via Asilo	NE	244
44.039	90	12.9	Turn right	Via degli Studi	SE	243
44.040	700	13.6	Pass a centro hippico and continue on the unmade road		E	241
44.041	300	13.9	Continue straight ahead	Towards the B&B	SE	244
44.042	130	14.0	Pass the B&B and turn right	Towards and to the left of the stone water fountain	S	245
44.043	80	14.1	Turn right	Keep the line of trees to your right	SW	241
44.044	200	14.3	Cross the channel, turn left	Beside another line	SE	236
44.045	600	14.9	Cross the channel and turn left	Poplar grove	NE	234
44.046	200	15.1	At the T-junction turn right on the track		SE	249
44.047	200	15.3	Continue straight ahead on the tarmac road		SE	247
44.048	300	15.6	At the junction with the main road turn left and immediately take via delle Guiette		N	243
44.049	300	15.9	Continue straight ahead on the paved road	Beside the channel	E	277
44.050	150	16.1	At the entrance to Piverone take the first road on the left		NE	296
44.051	60	16.1	At the T-junction turn left and the the first road to the right		N	304
44.052	100	16.2	Turn right	Via principale di Piverone	SE	308
44.053	200	16.4	Continue straight ahead	Pass beside the Piverone tower	SE	309

Ivrea to Santhià 37.9 km

Way Point N°	Way Point Distance (metres)	Total Distance (kilometres)	Directions	Verification Point	Compass	Altitude (metres)
44.054	100	16.5	In front of the church cross the road and continue straight ahead	Via Castellazzo	SE	307
44.055	400	16.9	After a section of tarmac continue straight ahead on a dirt road	Downhill	E	299
44.056	400	17.3	Beside a farm entrance take the track to the left		E	303
44.057	900	18.2	Beside the small ruined church of Gesiun turn left and immediately right	Towards the farm	SE	328
44.058	800	19.0	At the T-junction turn right	Views of lake Viverone	SW	321
44.059	110	19.1	At the junction with the tarmac road turn left		SE	315
44.060	200	19.3	Continue straight ahead on the unmade track	Beside farm	SE	312
44.061	200	19.5	Continue ahead on the tarmac		SE	312
44.062	600	20.1	Take the right fork		SE	309
44.063	600	20.7	Continue straight ahead into the town of Viverone	San Michele	S	289
44.064	300	21.0	At the Stop sign turn left	Via Umberto I	SE	277
44.065	800	21.8	Continue straight ahead in the direction of Roppolo	Church of San Rocco	SE	312
44.066	900	22.7	Continue straight ahead into Roppolo	Via Roma	SE	310
44.067	90	22.8	In the piazza turn left	Towards the castle	E	309
44.068	700	23.5	At the junction to Pioglio take the turning to the left		N	335
44.069	200	23.7	Take the road to the right	Direction Salomone	E	358

Way Point N°	Way Point Distance (metres)	Total Distance (kilometres)	Directions	Verification Point	Compass	Altitude (metres)
44.070	800	24.5	Pass the cemetery and after a brief climb ignore the first track to the right and a little after take the unmade road on the right across the hillside		S	364
44.071	1000	25.5	After descending on the track through fields and woods and arriving at a tarmac road turn left and then, immediately right		S	323
44.072	110	25.6	At a bend to the left continue straight ahead on the track		SW	307
44.073	200	25.8	At the T-junction turn left		SE	297
44.074	200	26.0	At the junction continue straight ahead	Near the sports ground	SE	289
44.075	300	26.3	At the Stop sign turn right		S	276
44.076	80	26.4	Turn left	Towards the centre	E	277
44.077	300	26.7	Turn left and then immediately right		E	272
44.078	150	26.9	Bear right on Strada Vicinale della Crocetta		SE	269
44.079	300	27.1	Follow the track straight ahead until T- junction and then continue straight		E	261
44.080	300	27.4	At the T-junction at the bottom of the road turn right	Santuario di N.S. del Babilone to the left	S	258
44.081	300	27.8	At the T-junction turn left		SE	256
44.082	600	28.4	At the T-junction turn left	Towards Cascina Maggiora	NE	251
44.083	300	28.6	Take the next turning to the right		E	255
44.084	400	29.1	Cross the main road and take the tarmac road to the right	Direction 'Agriturismo il Molino	E	243

Ivrea to Santhià 37.9 km

Way Point N°	Way Point Distance (metres)	Total Distance (kilometres)	Directions	Verification Point	Compass	Altitude (metres)
44.085	1400	30.4	Take the track to the right	After descending towards Cascina Biglia	E	239
44.086	400	30.9	Continue straight ahead at the junction in the woods		E	233
44.087	700	31.6	Cross a small bridge and continue straight ahead		S	218
44.088	200	31.8	Continue straight ahead along the old road	Ignore the turning to the left	S	218
44.089	400	32.1	Continue straight ahead		S	213
44.090	700	32.9	At the crossroads turn left	Towards the motorway bridge	E	209
44.091	200	33.0	Cross over the motorway		SE	205
44.092	400	33.5	Immediately after the bridge turn right		N	202
44.093	160	33.6	At the T-junction turn right		NE	202
44.094	200	33.8	Turn right		SE	201
44.095	800	34.6	At the crossroads continue straight ahead	Beside farm	E	196
44.096	400	35.0	Take the right fork	Towards electricity pylon	SE	190
44.097	1000	36.0	Pass a farm and a sharp left bend and continue ahead on the track		S	186
44.098	700	36.7	At the T-junction turn left		SE	185
44.099	300	37.0	At the first road junction turn right		S	186
44.100	140	37.1	Cross the Santhià ring road and continue straight ahead	Towards the centre of the town	S	186
44.101	500	37.6	At the traffic lights go straight ahead	Via Svizzera	S	187
44.102	80	37.7	Turn left	Via De Amicis	E	188
44.103	50	37.8	Turn right	Towards piazza Roma	SE	187
44.104	80	37.9	Arrive in Santhià centre	Beside the church		188

Vercelli is a city of about 50,000 inhabitants and one of the oldest urban sites in northern Italy, founded, according to most historians, around 600 BC. The world's first University funded by public money was established in 1228 in Vercelli and today the city still has a university of Literature and Philosophy as a part of the Università del Piemonte Orientale. Originally a Roman town and later a prosperous free commune, Vercelli passed to the Visconti of Milan in 1335 and was ceded by them to the house of Savoy in 1427.

Main sights

Vercelli is home to numerous relics of the Roman period: an amphitheatre, hippodrome, sarcophagi and many important inscriptions, some of which are Christian. There are also two noteworthy towers: the Torre dell'Angelo and the Torre di Città in via Gioberti. The Cathedral, formerly adorned with precious pillars and mosaics, was erected and enlarged by St Eusebius of Vercelli, to whom it was dedicated after his death. It was remodelled in the ninth century, and radically changed in the sixteenth by Count Alfieri. Like the other churches in the city it contains valuable paintings, especially those of Gaudenzio Ferrari, Gerolamo Giovenone and Lanino, who were natives of Vercelli. The cathedral library holds the famous Vercelli Book—an Old English manuscript which includes the celebrated alliterative poem The Dream of the Rood, the 8th century Laws of the Lombards and other early manuscripts. The Basilica di Sant'Andre, erected by Cardinal Guala Bicchieri in 1219 and the Cistercian monastery, one of the most beautiful and best preserved Romanesque monuments in Italy.

Santhià to Vercelli 27.8 km

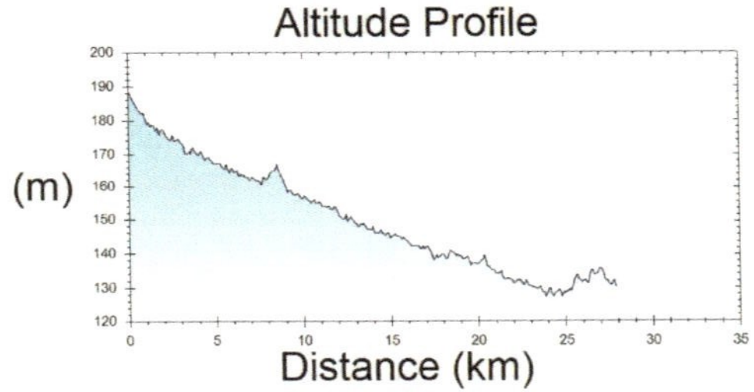

Route Summary: this section meanders on farm tracks between rice fields occasionally crossing the busy main road. When it is hot and damp the area is a haven for mosquitoes.

Distance from Canterbury: 1213km **Distance to Rome:** 863km

Ascent: 67m **Descent:** 130m

Way Point N°	Way Point Distance (metres)	Total Distance (kilometres)	Directions	Verification Point	Compass	Altitude (metres)
45.001	0	0.0	Leave piazza Roma keeping the church to the left		S	195
45.002	50	0.1	At the T-junction turn left	Pedestrian zone – corso Nuova Italia	E	188
45.003	600	0.7	Join the cycle path and cross the railway on the foot-bridge		SE	182
45.004	70	0.7	After crossing the bridge, continue straight ahead on the pavement on the left-side of the tarmac road	Corso Vercelli, large irrigation channel on the right	E	182
45.005	400	1.1	Just before the chapel, cross to the right side of the road and go straight ahead on the busy SS143	Keep water to the right	E	179
45.006	300	1.4	Carefully cross the main road and turn left over the small bridge	Via Pragilardo towards railway line	NE	177
45.007	400	1.8	After crossing the railway bridge bear right on the unmade road		E	176
45.008	1800	3.6	After passing cascina Pragilardo turn right	Beside electricity sub-station	S	170
45.009	500	4.1	At the T-junction turn left		E	168
45.010	700	4.8	At the crossroads continue straight ahead on the white road		E	167

Santhià to Vercelli 27.8 km

Way Point N°	Way Point Distance (metres)	Total Distance (kilometres)	Directions	Verification Point	Compass	Altitude (metres)
45.011	600	5.4	After crossing the Cavour canal turn right	Proceed with canal on the right	S	165
45.012	1000	6.4	Bear left beside the railway track	Railway on the right, before the track turns to the left	NE	163
45.013	400	6.8	Take the next right turn	Parallel to the railway	E	163
45.014	400	7.2	Cross the tarmac road and continue ahead on the grass track		E	162
45.015	60	7.3	At the T-junction turn right and keep to the left side of the road	Towards the village of San Germano Vercellese	SE	162
45.016	400	7.7	At the junction turn right under the railway	Towards the centre of the town	SE	163
45.017	70	7.8	In front of the railway station turn left towards the centre of the town	Piazzale P.Perazzo	SW	163
45.018	100	7.8	Continue straight ahead	Towards the porticos, Via Modesto Cugnolio	SW	164
45.019	200	8.1	At the crossroads turn left	Via Cavour	SE	165
45.020	140	8.2	Continue straight ahead across the piazza Giuseppe Mazzini	Beside the church	E	167
45.021	100	8.3	In piazza Garibaldi turn right	Towards the main road	S	165
45.022	80	8.4	Cross the main road and turn left	Keeping the café on your right	SE	164
45.023	100	8.5	Cross the small park and turn right	Cross the bridge over the canal	S	163
45.024	50	8.5	Immediately turn left on via Franzoi	Returning towards the main road	E	162
45.025	150	8.7	At the junction with the main road turn right on the smaller road	Towards Salasco	SE	160

Way Point N°	Way Point Distance (metres)	Total Distance (kilometres)	Directions	Verification Point	Compass	Altitude (metres)
45.026	500	9.2	On the exit from the town turn sharp left onto a track		E	158
45.027	400	9.6	At the crossroads turn left on the unmade road	Towards the main road	N	157
45.028	80	9.7	Cross the main road and turn left on the pavement		NW	156
45.029	90	9.7	Quickly turn right over the bridge and bear right on the track away from the main road		E	157
45.030	1100	10.8	At the crossroads continue straight ahead	Towards the railway and keeping the railway to the left	E	154
45.031	1400	12.2	At the junction beside the railway bridge continue straight ahead	Keep railway to the left before the track bears right beside the irrigation channel	SE	151
45.032	1600	13.8	At the junction continue straight ahead	Remain beside the irrigation channel	SE	147
45.033	500	14.3	At cascina Castellone turn right	Keep the farm buildings on the left	S	147
45.034	120	14.5	At the entrance to the farm buildings turn right	Towards the main road	SW	146
45.035	400	14.9	Cross the main road and turn left on the unmade road	Beside the main road	SE	145
45.036	70	14.9	Follow the unmade road to the right	Away from the main road	S	145
45.037	200	15.1	Continue straight ahead past the barrier		S	146
45.038	200	15.3	At the next crossroads turn left		E	145

Way Point N°	Way Point Distance (metres)	Total Distance (kilometres)	Directions	Verification Point	Compass	Altitude (metres)
45.039	900	16.2	At the T-junction turn left	After the junction the track quickly bears right	E	142
45.040	400	16.6	At the junction with the tarmac road turn left on the road	Towards the main road	NE	142
45.041	180	16.8	Just before reaching the main road turn right on the track		SE	142
45.042	600	17.4	At the junction with the tarmac road turn right on the road		S	139
45.043	1400	18.8	At the crossroads beside the Sali Vercellese cemetery turn left on the tree lined road	Towards Montonero	E	139
45.044	1200	20.0	Continue straight ahead towards Montonero		E	137
45.045	140	20.1	Continue straight ahead on the tarmac road		E	138
45.046	300	20.4	Pass through the village and continue straight ahead on the unmade road		E	137
45.047	300	20.8	Continue straight ahead	Ignore the turning to the right	E	135
45.048	140	20.9	Continue straight ahead	Ignore the turning to the left	E	135
45.049	1300	22.2	At the T-junction turn right		S	131
45.050	170	22.4	Cross a sluice gate and a small bridge and follow the embankment to the left		E	132
45.051	200	22.6	Cross a sluice-gate and continue straight ahead		E	131
45.052	800	23.4	Continue straight ahead	Pass a farm on the right	NE	129

Way Point N°	Way Point Distance (metres)	Total Distance (kilometres)	Directions	Verification Point	Compass	Altitude (metres)
45.053	110	23.5	Continue straight ahead	On the embankment	NE	130
45.054	100	23.6	Continue straight ahead beside the waterway	The track widens	SE	130
45.055	500	24.1	At the T-junction turn left on the cart track		NE	130
45.056	300	24.4	Continue straight ahead	Cross the barrier	E	127
45.057	400	24.8	Cross the main road and continue straight ahead	Towards the Vercelli ring-road	E	128
45.058	500	25.3	At the T-junction with the tarmac road turn right	The road quickly bears left	E	129
45.059	300	25.6	At the roundabout continue straight ahead		E	132
45.060	200	25.8	At the next roundabout again continue straight ahead		E	133
45.061	70	25.8	Immediately bear right	Via Giacomo Puccini	E	132
45.062	200	26.0	At the T-junction turn right	Railway to the left	S	132
45.063	90	26.1	Turn left under the railway and continue straight ahead	Via Trino	NE	131
45.064	400	26.5	At the roundabout bear left	Direction il Centro	N	135
45.065	400	26.9	At the roundabout bear left on via Fiume	In the direction of the railway station	NW	135
45.066	500	27.4	In piazza Martiri della Libertà turn right	Corso Giovanni Gastaldi	NE	132
45.067	170	27.6	At the roundabout continue straight ahead		NE	131
45.068	200	27.8	Arrive Vercelli centre	Piazza Roma	NW	132

Hotel/B&B	Price
Hotel Croce di Malta, 2, C.so Marcello Prestinari - 13100 VERCELLI Tel: 0039 (0)161 214432	B2
Cascina Erbade, Strada Boarone - 13100 VERCELLI Tel: 0039 (0)161 213656 www.grafhardenberg.eu hardenberg@tiscali.it	B2
Hotel Delle Miniere , 91, corso Matteotti - 13047 SAN GERMANO VERCELLESE Tel: 0039 (0)161 933111	B2
Karola Gräfin von Hardenberg, Cascina Erbade - 13100 VERCELLI Tel: 0039 (0)161 213656 hardenberg@tiscali.it	B1

Religious Hostel	Price
Monastero Sta Chiara, 10, via Feliciano da Gattinara - 13100 VERCELLI Tel: 0039 (0)161 860511	B2
Monastero S.TA Chiara, 10, via Feliciano da Gattinara - 13100 VERCELLI Tel: 0039 (0)163 860511	Donation
Arcivescovile Seminary, 10, piazza Sant Eusebio - 13100 VERCELLI Tel: 0039 (0)161 255550	Donation

Equestrian

Vola Ranch, Cascina Vola - 16100 VERCELLI Mobile: 0039 347 7669928
lola_ippicavola@libero.it **Note:** Approximately 4km outside Vercelli

Useful Contacts

Tourist/Information Office

Agenzia Turistica Locale, 90, viale Garibaldi - 13100 VERCELLi
Tel: 0039 (0)161 58002 www.atlvalsesiavercelli.it infovercelli@atlvalsesiavercelli.it

Doctor

Dr. Luigi E Paola, 27, via Duchessa Iolanda - 13100 VERCELLI
Tel: 0039 (0)161 253325

Veterinary

Avalle Dr. Luisa, 2, via Ferrari Gaudenzio - 13100 VERCELLI
Tel: 0039 (0)161 51657

Farrier

La Bottega Del Fabbro Di Grasso Carmine, via Manzone Walter - 13100 VERCELLI Tel: 0039 (0)161 602784

Stage	Length (m)	Scale	Supplier #1	Name #1	Reference #1
Besançon to Etalans	28520	1:25,000	IGN	Besançon/Forét de Chalezeule	3323ET
		1:25,000	IGN	Ornans/Source de la Loue	3424OT
Etalans to Ouhans	29010	1:25,000	IGN	Ornans/Source de la Loue	3424OT
Ouhans to Pontarlier	17680	1:25,000	IGN	Ornans/Source de la Loue	3424OT
		1:25,000	IGN	Pontarlier/Lac de Saint-Point	3425OT
Pontarlier to St Croix	23310	1:25,000	IGN	Pontarlier/Lac de Saint-Point	3425OT
		1:25,000	Kümmerly + Frey	Neuchâtel / Val de Travers / Lac de Morat	978-3-259-00878-2 08
Sainte-Croix to Orbe	35480	1:60000	Kümmerly + Frey	Neuchâtel / Val de Travers / Lac de Morat	978-3-259-00878-2 08
		1:60000	Kümmerly + Frey	Lausanne/ Vallée de Joux	978-3-259-00899-7 15
Orbe to Lausanne	38150	1:60000	Kümmerly + Frey	Lausanne/ Vallée de Joux	978-3-259-00899-7 15
Lausanne to Villeneuve	34710	1:60000	Kümmerly + Frey	Lausanne/ Vallée de Joux	978-3-259-00899-7 15
Villeneuve to Martigny	40160	1:60000	Kümmerly + Frey	Grand-St-Bernard / Dents du Midi / Les Diablerets	978-3-259-00828-7 22
Martigny **to Orsières**	20170	1:60000	Kümmerly + Frey	Grand-St-Bernard / Dents du Midi / Les Diablerets	978-3-259-00828-7 22
Orsières to col Grand Saint Bernard	25740	1:60000	Kümmerly + Frey	Grand-St-Bernard / Dents du Midi / Les Diablerets	978-3-259-00828-7 22

Stage	Length (m)	Scale	Supplier #1
Summit of the Great St Bernard Pass to Gignod	Carta topografica d'Italia serie 1:50,000	Foglio 090	AOSTA Edizione/aggiornamento anno 1996
Gignod to Chatillon	Carta topografica d'Italia serie 1:50,000	Foglio 090	AOSTA Edizione/aggiornamento anno 1996
Chatillon to Pont Saint Martin	Carta topografica d'Italia serie 1:50,000	Foglio 091	CHATILLON Edizione/aggiornamento anno 1996
	Carta topografica d'Italia serie 1:50,000	Foglio 092	VERRES Edizione/aggiornamento anno 1996
Pont Saint Martin **to Ivrea**	Carta topografica d'Italia serie 1:50,000	Foglio 092	VERRES Edizione/aggiornamento anno 1996
	Carta topografica d'Italia serie 1:50,000	Foglio 092	IVREA Edizione/aggiornamento anno 1998
Ivrea to Santhia	Carta topografica d'Italia serie 1:50,000	Foglio 114	IVREA Edizione/aggiornamento anno 1998
	Carta topografica d'Italia serie 1:50,000	Foglio 115	BIELLA Edizione/aggiornamento anno 1998
Santhia to Vercelli	Carta topografica d'Italia serie 1:50,000	Foglio 136	SANTHIA Edizione/aggiornamento anno 1974
	Carta topografica d'Italia serie 1:50,000	Foglio 136	SANTHIA Edizione/aggiornamento anno 1974
	Carta topografica d'Italia serie 1:50,000	Foglio 137	VERCELLI currently out of print

The list below gives details of the churches and religious organisations either in or near towns along the route. These have not specifically stated that accommodation is provided for pilgrims, but it is likely that a phone call will put you in contact with someone who will be able/willing to help. Note: * indicates that there are more churches than could be listed in this limited space

BESANCON	Association Diocésaine Sacré Cœur, 14 av Carnot 25000 BESANCON Tel: 0033 (0)3 81 80 90 55
	Association Diocésaine Saint Pierre, 10 pl 8 Septembre 25000 BESANCON Tel: 0033 (0)3 81 82 02 45
	Association Diocésaine, 23 r Eglise 25000 BESANCON Tel: 0033 (0)3 81 80 27 70
	Association du Rosaire, 30 r Fontenottes 25000 BESANCON Tel: 0033 (0)3 81 52 98 53
	Association Diocésaine Notre Dame du Foyer, 55 r Chasnot 25000 BESANCON Tel: 0033 (0)3 81 88 64 85
	Soeurs de la Charité, 131 Grande rue 25000 BESANCON Tel: 0033 (0)3 81 82 00 89
	Monastère de Ste Claire, 6 r Chapitre 25000 BESANCON Tel: 0033 (0)3 81 82 10 25
	Les Franciscains, chem Chapelle des Buis 25000 BESANCON Tel: 0033 (0)3 81 81 33 25
ETALANS	Presbytère, 23 Grande rue 25580 ETALANS Tel: 0033 (0)3 81 59 20 54
OUHANS	Presbytère, 17 Grande rue 25520 GOUX LES USIERS Tel: 0033 (0)3 81 38 21 14 **Note:** 3km from Ouhans
PONTARLIER	Cure de Saint Pierre, 8 Bis r Capit Bulle 25300 PONTARLIER Tel: 0033 (0)3 81 46 83 48
SWITZERLAND	
LAUSANNE	International Evangelical Church, Place de la Riponne 7 CH-1005 Lausanne Tel: 0041 (0)24 453 21 10
	Lausanne Free Church, chemin des Fleurettes 36 1007 Lausanne paula.hill@gmail.com
	Christ Church, avenue de l'Eglise Anglaise, Case Postale 70, CH 1000 Tel: 0041 (0)21 617 7670
MARTIGNY	Evangélique de Réveil, rue de la Moya 1 1920 Martigny Tel: 0041 (0)27 746 43 89 Mobile 0041 (0)79 774 61 19
	Néo-apostolique de Suisse, avenue de la Gare 45 1920 Martigny Tel: 0041 (0)27 723 38 43

AOSTA

	2 Parrocchia Della Cattedrale, 4, via Conte Tommaso 11100 Aosta (AO) Tel: 0039 (0)165 40251
	Parrocchia Di San Lorenzo, 1, via Rey Guido 11100 Aosta (AO) Tel: 0039 (0)165 236552
	Oratorio Saint Martin, 1, viale Europa 11100 Aosta (AO) Tel: 0039 (0)165 554234
	Parrocchia Di Santo'Orso, 14, via S. Orso 11100 Aosta (AO) Tel: 0039 (0)165 262026
CHATILLON	Parrocchia Di Chatillon, via Gervasone Adolfo 11024 Chatillon (AO) Tel: 0039 (0)166 563040
PONT-SAINT-MARTIN	Parrocchia S. Lorenzo, 4, via S. Lorenzo 11026 Pont-saint-martin (AO) Tel: 0039 (0)125 807061
IVREA	Chiesa Del Sacro Cuore Di Gesu', 11, Cantone Maridon 10015 Ivrea (TO) Tel: 0039 (0)125 234219
	Chiesa Ss. Salvatore, 45, via Palestro 10015 Ivrea (TO) Tel: 0039 (0)125 45038
	Curia Vescovile Abitazione Del Vescovo, 3, piazza Castello 10015 Ivrea (TO) Tel: 0039 (0)125 641380
	Curia Vescovile Istituto Diocesano Sostent, 3, piazza Castello 10015 Ivrea (TO) Tel: 0039 (0)125 424604
	Diocesi Di Ivrea Istituto Scienze Religiose, 9, via s. Varmondo Arborio 10015 Ivrea (TO) Tel: 0039 (0)125 627422
	Oratorio San Giuseppe, 6, via s. Varmondo Arborio 10015 Ivrea (TO) Tel: 0039 (0)125 641462
VERCELLI *	Basilica Di Sant'Andrea, 35, piazza Roma 13100 Vercelli (VC) Tel: 0039 (0)161 255513

The Pilgrim Record (also known as Pilgrim Passport or Pilgrim Credential) is a certificate of pilgrim status, and may be required for access to pilgrim accommodation. It is stamped at the beginning of your journey, and daily at Churches, town halls, bars etc along the way. Pilgrim records are made available only to walkers, cyclists, and pilgrims on horseback.
Download version also available from:
www.pilgrimagepublications.com

The longest journey begins with a single step.

Lao Tzu

Name:	
Address:	
Date Started:	
Place Started:	
Date Ended:	
Signature:	
Horse:	
Bicycle:	
On Foot:	

Pilgrim record - Signature & Stamp	Pilgrim record - Signature & Stamp
Pilgrim record - Signature & Stamp	Pilgrim record - Signature & Stamp

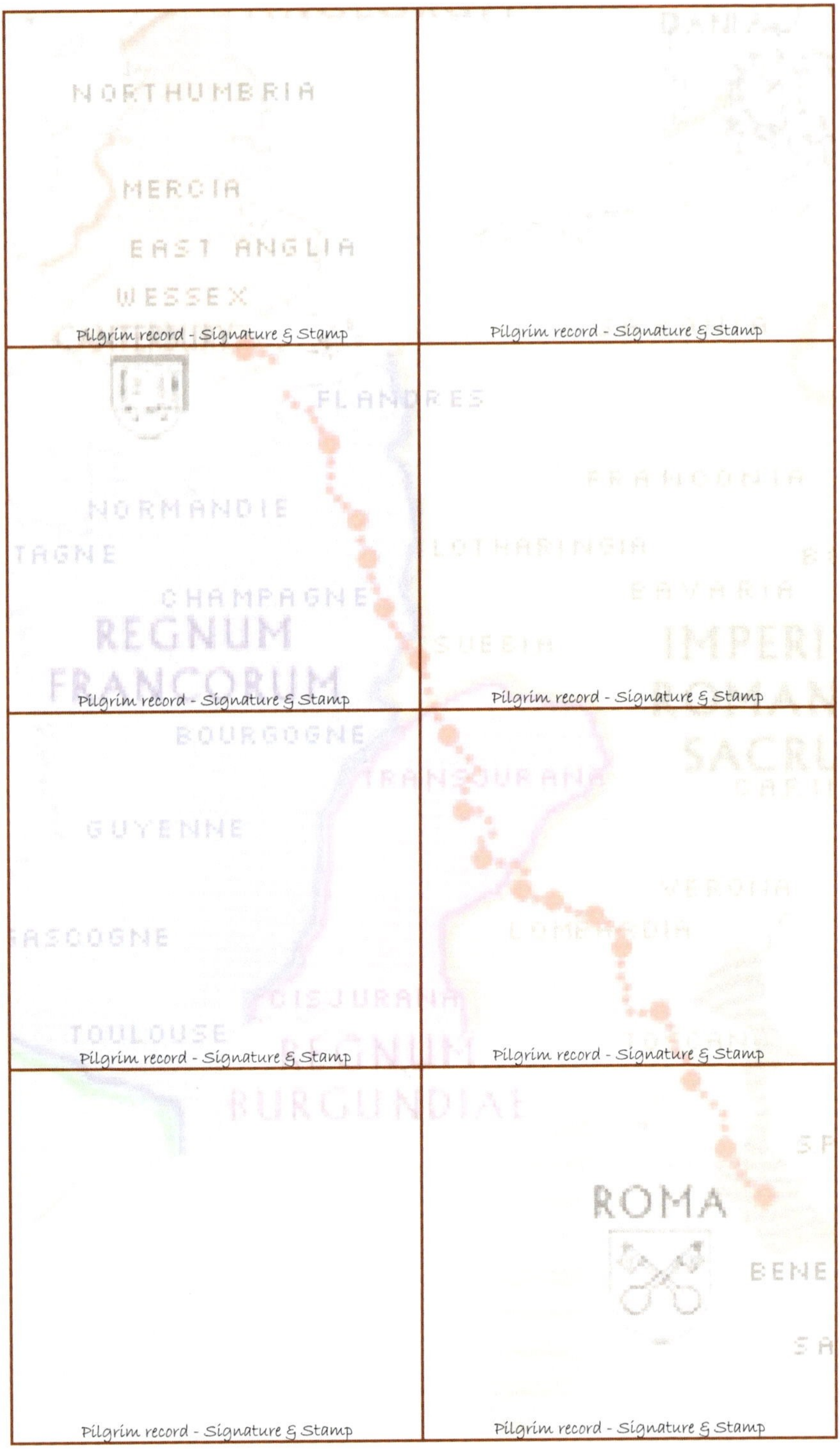

Pilgrim record - Signature & Stamp	Pilgrim record - Signature & Stamp
Pilgrim record - Signature & Stamp	Pilgrim record - Signature & Stamp
Pilgrim record - Signature & Stamp	Pilgrim record - Signature & Stamp
Pilgrim record - Signature & Stamp	Pilgrim record - Signature & Stamp

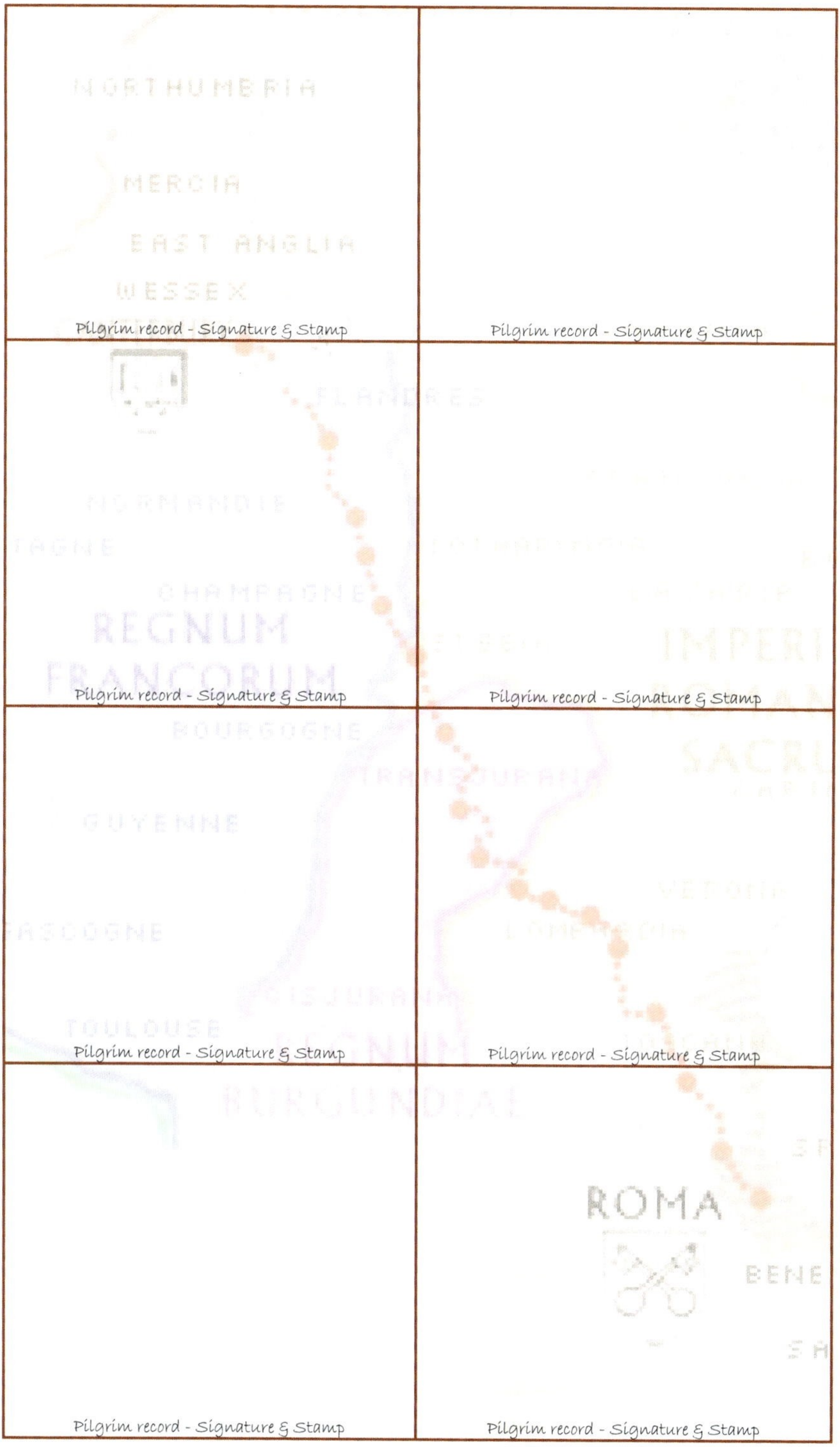

Pilgrim record - Signature & Stamp	Pilgrim record - Signature & Stamp
Pilgrim record - Signature & Stamp	Pilgrim record - Signature & Stamp
Pilgrim record - Signature & Stamp	Pilgrim record - Signature & Stamp
Pilgrim record - Signature & Stamp	Pilgrim record - Signature & Stamp

Pilgrim record - Signature & Stamp	Pilgrim record - Signature & Stamp
Pilgrim record - Signature & Stamp	Pilgrim record - Signature & Stamp
Pilgrim record - Signature & Stamp	Pilgrim record - Signature & Stamp
Pilgrim record - Signature & Stamp	Pilgrim record - Signature & Stamp

Pilgrim record - Signature & Stamp	Pilgrim record - Signature & Stamp
Pilgrim record - Signature & Stamp	Pilgrim record - Signature & Stamp
Pilgrim record - Signature & Stamp	Pilgrim record - Signature & Stamp
Pilgrim record - Signature & Stamp	Pilgrim record - Signature & Stamp

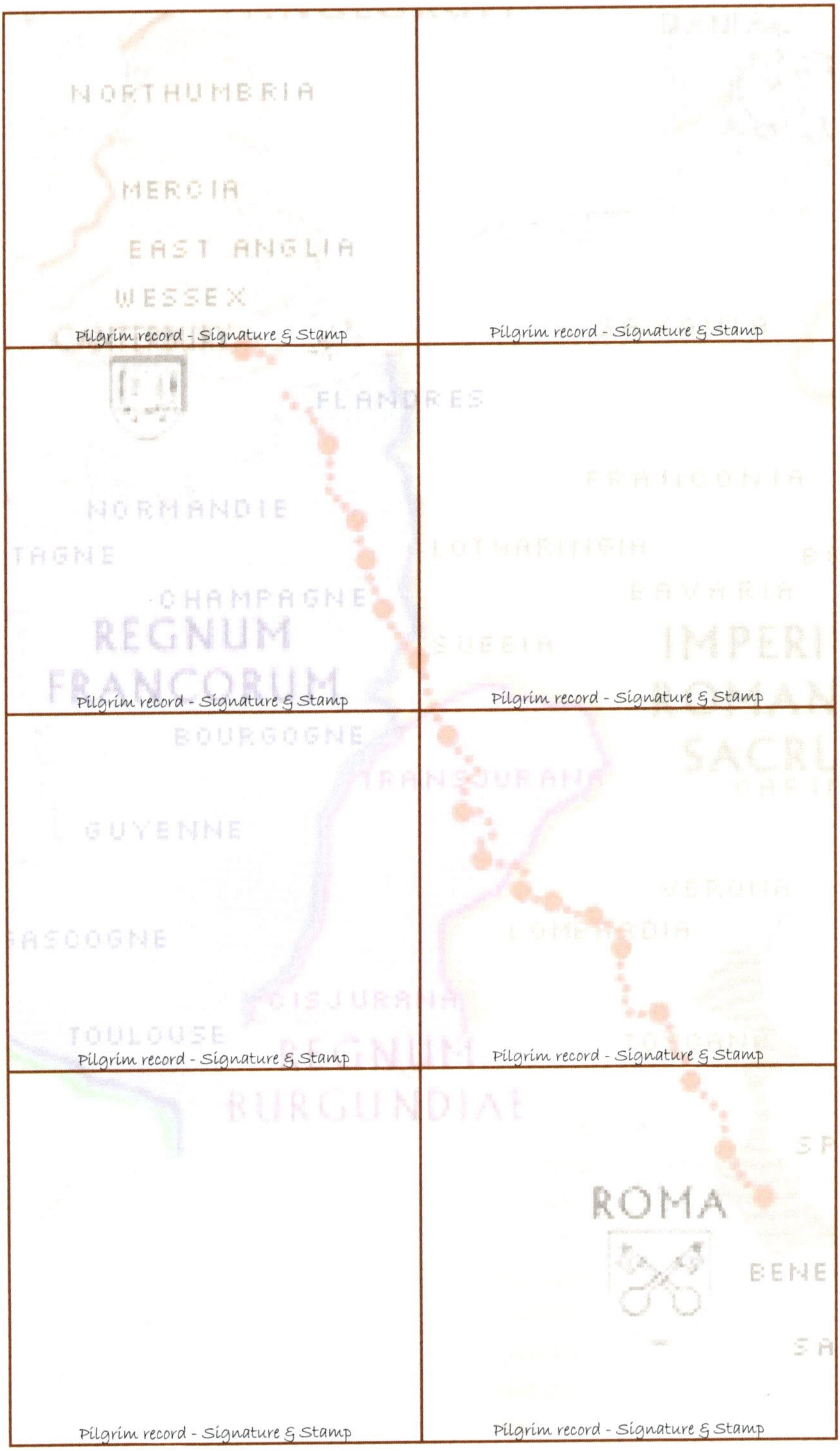

Pilgrim record - Signature & Stamp	Pilgrim record - Signature & Stamp
Pilgrim record - Signature & Stamp	Pilgrim record - Signature & Stamp
Pilgrim record - Signature & Stamp	Pilgrim record - Signature & Stamp
Pilgrim record - Signature & Stamp	Pilgrim record - Signature & Stamp

the bill IT il conto

LaVergne, TN USA
25 March 2010
1742LVUK00001B

9782917183076